THE CASE FOR EFFECTIVE LEGAL WRITING

The Case for Effective Legal Writing

Court Opinions, Commentary, and Exercises

DIANA J. SIMON
ASSOCIATE CLINICAL PROFESSOR OF LAW
JAMES E. ROGERS COLLEGE OF LAW
UNIVERSITY OF ARIZONA

MARK COONEY
PROFESSOR OF LAW
THOMAS M. COOLEY LAW SCHOOL

CAROLINA ACADEMIC PRESS
Durham, North Carolina

LIBRARY OF CONGRESS CATALOGING-IN-PUBLICATION DATA

Names: Simon, Diana J., author. | Cooney, Mark, author.
Title: The case for effective legal writing : court opinions, commentary, and exercises / Diana J. Simon and Mark Cooney.
Description: Durham, North Carolina : Carolina Academic Press, 2024. | Includes bibliographical references and index.
Identifiers: LCCN 2024000030 | ISBN 9781531028336 (paperback) | ISBN 9781531028343 (ebook)
Subjects: LCSH: Legal composition. | Legal composition--Problems, exercises, etc. | Law--Language. | Legal research. | LCGFT: Court decisions and opinions.
Classification: LCC KF250 .S533 2024 | DDC 808.06/634--dc23/eng/20240126
LC record available at https://lccn.loc.gov/2024000030

CAROLINA ACADEMIC PRESS
700 Kent Street
Durham, North Carolina 27701
(919) 489-7486
www.cap-press.com

Printed in the United States of America

Contents

About the Authors

This book's authors are endlessly fascinated by lawyering and legal language. Between them, they spent more than 30 years in private practice and saw firsthand how legal writing impacts every aspect of the law. They've also spent more than a combined 40 years helping students grow into standout legal writers and lawyers. Their great joy has been to watch that growth and to play some role in nurturing it.

Diana J. Simon is Associate Clinical Professor of Law at the University of Arizona's James E. Rogers College of Law. She is author of *The (Not Too Serious) Grammar, Punctuation, and Style Guide to Legal Writing* (Carolina Academic Press 2022). Her articles have appeared or are forthcoming in the *Charleston Law Review, Duquesne Law Review, Legal Communication & Rhetoric: JALWD*, and elsewhere. She is Managing Editor of the *Journal of Appellate Practice and Process* and won the Global Legal Skills Award for scholarship on cross-cultural education in 2019. Before teaching full time, she practiced for 23 years, focusing on commercial litigation.

Mark Cooney is a Professor and Chairs the Research & Writing Department at Thomas M. Cooley Law School. He was Editor in Chief of *The Scribes Journal of Legal Writing* for six volumes and now serves as a Senior Editor. He is author of *Sketches on Legal Style* (Carolina Academic Press 2013) and has published more than 50 articles or book chapters on legal writing and other topics. His works have appeared in *The Green Bag*, *Legal Communication & Rhetoric: JALWD*, the *Scribes Journal*, and elsewhere, and have been quoted and cited by state and federal courts.

Preface

Why devote yourself to legal writing?

In law school, you'll learn how to "write like a lawyer." We hope so. And we hope not. The phrase *legal writing* carries both import and baggage. For all its potential to foster positive change and embody our best ideals, legal writing has drawn scorn. When most people think of legal writing, they likely picture fine print (hiding trap doors), bloated legalese, dense walls of text with only occasional indents, and so on. Indeed, legal writing's reputation has suffered since our nation's founding. But exceptional legal writers have emerged along the way—writers admired for their lucidity. You can be one of them.

So let's get practical and talk about what legal writing means to you. What about your future, your career? Will it matter whether you impress readers? Let's give it some thought. Besides opposing attorneys assessing your arguments (and skill), when you write in the legal profession, your readers will be:

- potential employers considering whether to hire you;
- employers paying your salary and assessing your worth;
- clients paying you hundreds of dollars per hour to write;
- vulnerable parties depending on you for effective representation;
- constituencies or other public interest groups working toward a common goal;

- judicial clerks recommending how your case/issue should be decided; and
- judges deciding your case.

Important readers, indeed. You'll want their good opinion. You'll want them to praise and value your work. You'll want them to be persuaded and find you credible. In short, you'll want them to feel a bond of goodwill with you. That's a bond that forms if, and only if, you have taken pains to do every part of your job—writing included—well.

Writing well takes time. It's not easy. But you can do it with dedication, and it's worth the effort. Every time you put fingers to keypad, think about a person on the above list. Imagine sitting next to them while they're reading your document, processing what's on your page. Let yourself feel that sense of shaky optimism. If you do that—if you constantly think about your reader while you write—you'll already be ahead of many practicing lawyers.

Why a casebook approach?

Among the many topics covered in your legal-writing courses will be style, grammar, and punctuation. And you may wonder why you're learning techniques that you covered in grade school. The reasons are simple.

The rules of writing are challenging and require lifelong attention. Those rules are as multifold and nuanced as the legal rules you'll learn in other courses. Besides that, lawyers, even experienced lawyers, often struggle with their writing and ignore the advice of legal-writing experts. Some of those lawyers have (as you'll soon see) suffered courts' wrath because of it. Courts and clients expend substantial resources resolving issues caused or clouded by thoughtless writing.

So the purpose of this casebook is two-fold: (1) to guide and instruct you on getting it right in your own writing; and (2) to demonstrate that writing style and mechanics should not be afterthoughts. We want you to see that style and mechanics are essential to effective legal writing and effective lawyering. Failing to master these skills can have legal or professional consequences.

Our choice of a casebook method for teaching you these skills is unusual—unique, even. We know of no other casebook on legal writing. But we see value in changing that. Rather than listing a set of writing techniques for you to follow without context, we're giving you examples of court cases that hinged, in whole or in part, on the quality of a legal writer's work product. In other words, this book will connect technique to real-world consequences.

Above all, we hope and believe that this book will prompt rich and useful conversations in and out of the classroom. And if we allow ourselves a fanciful wish, we hope that experiencing this material in a casebook format, with the attendant drama of actual cases, will spark some readers to become true legal-writing fanatics (like us).

What should you know about the selected cases?

We've tried to select interesting cases. And we've tried our best to avoid areas of law that pose extra layers of complexity, such as tax law or secured transactions. We've also tried to avoid cases that address especially sensitive issues, such as sexual assault or other acts of violence and cruelty.

We've tried to use recent cases, too. Almost all our principal cases were decided after 2000, and many, if not most, are newer than 2010. A fair number are from the 2020s. Our aim was to capture the current state of the law and the profession. But you'll spot a few older cases.

We have heavily edited the cases for succinctness and readability. Courts and authors often augment citations with parenthetical notes acknowledging that they've "cleaned up" the quoted passage. Well, we've done *lots* of cleaning. Among other things, we've often altered or removed footnotes, citations, bracketed notes, parentheses, italics, and multi-level quotation marks. We've also unbolded courts' headings to avoid confusion with this book's section and subsection headings. In just a few places, we've made other minor alterations for flow, consistency, or clarity.

We also didn't want our principal cases to be burdensome. Thus, what you'll see here is heavily truncated. We have a chapter on the ills of verbosity, and we've tried to practice what we've preached.

A final but important point: we've avoided cases in which the offending legal writer was a *pro se* litigant. Learning the fate of untrained lay writers would muddy our message and do little to inspire law students to dedicate themselves to their craft.

And with that, welcome to a textbook that brings the courthouse to the legal-writing classroom.

Acknowledgments

Diana Simon would like to thank Susie Salmon, director of the legal writing program at the University of Arizona College of Law. Susie encouraged her to write a book full of case excerpts to illustrate the consequences of poor legal writing. She would like to thank Mark Cooney for saying yes when she asked him to be a coauthor. She would also like to thank her research assistant, Molly Case. Molly not only reviewed and corrected every footnote, but she also gave valuable editing suggestions and offered the critical perspective that only a law student can provide. Finally, she would like to thank her husband, Don Tringali, a transactional lawyer, for offering his insight and for his ever-present support and encouragement.

Mark Cooney would like to thank his coauthor, Diana Simon, for letting him elbow his way into this project. This book wouldn't exist but for her vision, leadership, and tireless productivity. He'd also like to thank his research assistant, Thomas McKee, whose work is unfailingly insightful, reliable, and precise. Thanks also to *The Scribes Journal of Legal Writing*, which published his article "Style Is Substance: Collected Cases Showing Why It Matters" in 2012. Some portions of that article have been revised, updated, and sprinkled into this book. Finally, he'd like to thank his daughters, Morgan and Maggie, whose remarkable accomplishments never cease to inspire him, and his wife, Lisa, who didn't balk at his long spells in the writing nook.

THE CASE FOR EFFECTIVE LEGAL WRITING

ONE

Effective Writing Is Effective Lawyering

A. Overview

Lawyers write. This is especially true for new lawyers. In fact, a 2013 study conducted by the National Conference of Bar Examiners showed that 100% of newly licensed attorneys reported needing to communicate in writing in their professional lives. When asked how significant written communication was to their overall performance, these new attorneys rated it a 3.77 out of 4—the highest rating reported.[1] The second-highest score was a 3.67 for "paying attention to the details."[2]

In 2018, a National Conference of Bar Examiners task force kicked off a comprehensive three-year study designed to ensure that the bar exam tests the knowledge and skills needed for competent entry-level legal practice in a changing profession.[3] In recognition of their being ranked as critical skills by

1. Susan M. Case, *The Testing Column: The NCBE Job Analysis: A Study of the Newly Licensed Lawyer*, 82 Bar Examiner 52–56 (March 2013), https://thebarexaminer.ncbex.org/wp-content/uploads/PDFs/820113testingcolumn.pdf.

2. *Id.* at 55.

3. National Conference of Bar Examiners, *Final Report of the Testing Task Force* 2 (April 2021), https://nextgenbarexam.ncbex.org/wp-content/uploads/TTF-Final-Report-April-2021.pdf.

both new and experienced lawyers,[4] legal writing and drafting will play a more central role on the NextGen Bar Exam.[5]

Given all this, you've probably been told that legal writing is important to your success as a lawyer. But you might not know that misusing grammar, punctuation, and other stylistic elements can create negative consequences for lawyers, their clients, and the justice system. In legal writing, the details matter. Style is not icing on the cake—style is the icing, the cake, the candles, and the goodie bag you take home after the party. Below is a preview of cases showing what happens when a lawyer's writing spoils the party.

B. Judges' Note to Lawyers: Go Back and Take Legal Writing

Judges know the importance of effective legal writing because it impacts them directly. They're often forced to decipher writing that makes little sense. Besides chastising lawyers whose writing is unintelligible, courts have dismissed cases and sanctioned lawyers because of poor writing.

For instance, in a disciplinary action involving a bankruptcy lawyer, the Minnesota Supreme Court held that the lawyer should be reprimanded and required to complete a continuing-education program "of at least 10 hours in legal writing."[6] The court noted that the lawyer had repeatedly filed documents "rendered unintelligible by numerous spelling, grammatical, and typographical errors," and the flaws were so serious that his filings amounted to "incompetent representation."[7] Even though no client was harmed, the court focused on the harm to the profession and to the administration of law, explaining that "[p]ublic confidence in the legal system is shaken when... a lawyer's [writings]

---

4. *Id.* Phase 2 consisted of a nationwide practice-analysis survey completed by nearly 15,000 lawyers that provided a rich set of data on the work performed by newly licensed lawyers and the knowledge and skills they need to perform that work.

5. National Conference of Bar Examiners, *Content Scope Outlines for Public Comment* (April 2022), https://nextgenbarexam.ncbex.org/reports/preliminary-content-scope/. While many bar exams have long included written and practical components, the NextGen Bar Exam proposes prioritizing assessment of these foundational skills and de-emphasizing the outsized role memorization of legal doctrine has historically played.

6. In re Disciplinary Action Against Hawkins, 502 N.W.2d 770, 772 (Minn. 1993).

7. *Id.* at 770–71.

are so filled with spelling, grammatical, and typographical errors that they are virtually incomprehensible."[8]

But this type of judicial rebuke hasn't been limited to professional-discipline cases. Courts frequently express frustration over contracts drafted by transactional lawyers, who are notorious for recycling forms written in a dense, antiquated style. For instance, in *Bank of New York v. First Millennium, Inc.*,[9] a complex case involving multiple financial institutions and the Federal Deposit Insurance Corporation, a federal judge faced the daunting task of construing multiple transaction documents. When he read those documents to discern the parties' intent, he struggled because they were so "convoluted and opaque."[10] He quipped that had the drafters been students in a legal-writing class, they would not have fared well:

> Presumably the transaction documents were drafted by lawyers. The record does not reveal their number or identity. With all *due* respect (I emphasize the adjective), if those lawyers had been law students and submitted these documents as a final exercise in a Pass/Fail course on Clarity in Legal Writing, their grade would not begin with a "P."[11]

Litigators have drawn similar criticisms for sloppy or incomplete court documents. In a federal credit-reporting case, a district court granted a reporting agency's motion for summary judgment in part because the plaintiff's response was so poorly written.[12] Aside from the response's failure to address the arguments raised in the motion, the court, commenting on counsel's lack of clarity, emphasized that a "first-year law student who submitted this 'response' for a legal writing class would likely be encouraged to rethink his or her choice of career. To receive such a grossly incompetent effort from a practicing lawyer is appalling."[13]

---

8. *Id.* at 771.

9. 598 F. Supp. 2d 550, 551–52, 567–68 (S.D.N.Y. 2009), *aff'd*, 607 F.3d 905 (2d Cir. 2010).

10. *Id.* at 568.

11. *Id.*

12. Butler-Rance v. Providian Bancorp Servs., Inc., 2007 WL 2310114 (M.D. Fla. Aug. 9, 2007).

13. *Id.* at *2.

As you see, judicial readers aren't shy about voicing their frustrations. The First Circuit referred to one lawyer's brief as "nearly incomprehensible."[14] And the Seventh Circuit, after addressing one deficient aspect of an attorney's brief, characterized the rest of the brief as "similarly wretched."[15]

Poor legal writing might even jeopardize a criminal conviction, though convincing an appellate court to overturn a conviction because of poor grammar is a tall order for any defense attorney. Consider the convicted burglar who argued that his indictment was legally deficient because, if read literally and grammatically, it charged inanimate objects—not him—with the crime.[16] The Mississippi Supreme Court agreed with his grammatical argument (if not his legal one), remarking that if the justices were English teachers, the conviction would require reversal because the indictment "would receive an 'F' from every English teacher in the land."[17] The case is particularly noteworthy for its amusing dissection of the indictment and because the defendant employed the unusual tactic of hiring an English teacher as an expert witness:

Henderson v. State

445 So. 2d 1364 (Miss. 1984)

ROBERTSON, Justice, for the Court:

....

The primary issue presented on this appeal regards the legal adequacy of the indictment under which Henderson has been tried, convicted, and sentenced. That indictment, in pertinent part, reads as follows:

> The Grand Jurors for the State of Mississippi,... upon their oaths present: That Jacob Henderson... on the 15th day of May, A.D., 1982.
>
> The store building there situated, the property of Metro Auto Painting, Inc.,... in which store building was kept for sale or use valuable things, to-wit: goods, ware and merchandise unlawfully, feloniously and burglariously did break and enter, with intent the goods, wares and merchandise of said Metro Auto Painting then and there being in

14. In re Gonzalez, 795 F.3d 288, 290 (1st Cir. 2015).

15. Sambrano v. Mabus, 663 F.3d 879, 881 (7th Cir. 2011).

16. Henderson v. State, 445 So. 2d 1364 (Miss. 1984).

17. *Id.* at 1365.

> said store building unlawfully, feloniously and then and there being in said store building burglariously to take, steal and carry away; And
>
> One (1) Polaroid Land Camera,
>
> One (1) Realistic AM/FM Stereo Tuner
>
> One (1) Westminster AM/FM radio
>
> One (1) Metal Box and contents thereof, ...
>
> the property of the said Metro Auto Painting then and there being in said store building did then and there unlawfully, feloniously and burglariously take, steal and carry away the aforesaid property....

Henderson, no doubt offended, demurred. In support, he presented an expert witness, Ann Dreher, who had been a teacher of English for nine years. Ms. Dreher testified that, when read consistent with accepted rules of English grammar, the indictment did not charge Jacob Henderson with doing anything; rather it charged that goods, wares, and merchandise broke and entered the paint store. The trial judge overruled the objection and the motion, but not without reservation. He stated:

> [T]his same objection has been made numerous times.... [B]ut as far as I know no one has elected to appeal and I'm going to follow the decision whether it is grammatically correct or not. I have repeatedly begged for six years or five years for the district attorney not to use this form. It is very poor English. It is impossible English.... I again ask the district attorney not to use this form. It's archaic. Even Shakespeare could not understand the grammatical construction of this indictment. But the objection will be overruled.

....

In the trial court and on this appeal, Henderson insists that the meaning of the indictment may be obtained only within the strait jacket of accepted rules of grammatical construction of the English language. From this point of view, we are asked to examine the indictment and concentrate on the words "unlawfully, feloniously and burglariously did break and enter...." Who, we are asked, when the rules of good grammar are employed, did this alleged breaking and entering?

There are two possible answers (again, looking at the indictment as would an English teacher). "Goods, wares and merchandise" are the most obvious choice. Those nouns proximately precede the verb(s) "did break and enter" (separated only by the familiar string of adverbs "unlawfully, feloniously and burglariously"—the district attorney, like other lawyers, never uses one word when two or three will do just as well). Thus read, the indictment charges that Goods, wares, and merchandise, not Jacob Henderson, burglarized the Maaco Paint Shop on May 15, 1982.

More properly, however, the words "Goods, wares and merchandise" are seen as the tail end of a largely unintelligible effort to describe something else: the store building. A perceptive English grammarian would conclude that it is "the store building there situated…." which is charged with the burglary, for those words seem to constitute the subject of the nonsensical non-sentence we are charged to construe.

Even so, whether the indictment charges that "Goods, wares and merchandise" *or* "The store building there situated"… "unlawfully, feloniously and burglariously did break and enter…." matters not to Jacob Henderson. His point is merely that the indictment does *not* charge that *he* did the breaking and entering.

Were this a Court of nine English teachers, Henderson no doubt would prevail.

The indictment does contain at the outset the charge "That Jacob Henderson…on the 15th day of May, A.D., 1982." We have another non-sentence. The unmistakable period after 1982 is used by astute defense counsel to nail down the point—that the indictment fails to charge that Jacob Henderson did anything on May 15, 1982. Again, we must concede that grammatically speaking counsel is correct. The period after 1982 grammatically precludes the possibility that the indictment charges that Jacob Henderson did break and enter. Either the words "did break and enter" would have to precede the period, or the name Jacob Henderson would have to appear following it. Neither is the case.

Recognizing that the period is important, the State argues that in reality the indictment consists of one long sentence, written albeit in legalese instead of English. The State argues that "the period grammatically disjoined the first part of the sentence from the second," conceding that we are indeed confronted with "a patently inappropriate period." This, of course, prompts Henderson to analogize the state's argument to Lady Macbeth's famous "Out damned spot! Out, I say!" The retort would be telling in the classroom or in a court of the literati. Alas, it has meager force in a court of law.

With no little temerity, we insist that the correct statement of the question before this Court is: Does the indictment conform to the requirements of Rule 2.05, Uniform Criminal Rules of Circuit Court Practice. [We hold that it does.].

….

Establishment of a literate bar is a worthy aspiration. 'Tis without doubt a consummation devoutly to be wished. Its achievement, however, must be relegated to means other than reversal of criminal convictions justly and lawfully secured....

C. Case Dismissed

Although the district attorney in *Henderson* used criminally poor grammar and survived, other lawyers haven't been so fortunate; numerous cases have been dismissed because of ineffective writing.

Consider cases interpreting the Federal Rules of Civil Procedure. The rules require that a pleading contain "a short and plain statement of the claim."[18] The rationale behind this rule is to prevent judges and parties from having to "fish a gold coin from a bucket of mud."[19] While it might seem that writing a short and plain statement would be easier than writing a long and convoluted claim, lawyers often struggle with this directive.

For example, in *Hunt v. Caliber Home Loans, Inc.*, the court granted a motion to dismiss the third amended complaint (yes, the lawyer was given four tries), explaining that the complaint was "disjointed, unclear, and prolix."[20] And this time, the court dismissed it with prejudice, meaning no more chances. Similarly, in *Eberhardt v. Village of Tinley Park*, the trial court dismissed a complaint consisting of 110 pages, 675 numbered paragraphs, and 25 counts.[21] In so holding, the court noted that while length alone would not justify dismissal, when length was coupled with "unintelligibility," there was a legitimate reason for dismissal.[22]

Clarity was also an issue when a court dismissed a second amended complaint with prejudice in *Shapiro v. Unum Life Insurance Co.*[23] The court's decision was based not only on length (487 pages) but also on the "opacity

---

18. Fed. R. Civ. P. (8)(a)(2).

19. United States ex rel. Garst v. Lockheed-Martin Corp., 328 F.3d 374, 378 (7th Cir. 2003).

20. 2018 WL 10799004, at * 2 (S.D. Fla. Mar. 6, 2018).

21. 2020 WL 10618313, at *1 (N.D. Ill. Oct. 14, 2020).

22. *Id.*

23. 2018 WL 4868913, at *1.

of the writing."[24] To help illustrate the problem, the court quoted a 141-word sentence from the complaint. Although the court acknowledged that with an abundance of time, "charitable interpretation, and head-scratching," it might have been able to decipher the complaint, because it was the plaintiff's third try, dismissal was appropriate.[25]

The Fifth Circuit was especially creative—Shakespearean, even—in denouncing a plaintiff's failure to plead his case with brevity and clarity.[26] The court peppered its opinion with pointed headings that left no question about its view of the rambling pleadings: "The Pleadings: Gobbledygook"; "'Let Thy Speech Be Short, Comprehending Much in Few Words.'"[27] The plaintiff's pleadings and related papers were so long that they would have required a "hand truck or cart to move."[28] And the pleadings were "not plain either."[29] The Fifth Circuit reversed the trial court's outright dismissal to give the plaintiff's attorney another chance. But it enthusiastically agreed with the trial court's central finding that, even though liberality is called for when evaluating pleadings, "we stand liberality on its head by accepting 4,000 pages of chaotic legal jargon in lieu of a short and plain statement."[30]

In reaching this decision, the court emphasized Rule 8's purpose, which is "to eliminate prolixity in pleading and to achieve brevity, simplicity, and clarity."[31] It added that in 16th-century England, the lawyer who filed the initial pleadings would have been fair game for discipline, meted out as follows:

> [A]n English chancellor decided to make an example of a particularly prolix document filed in his court. The chancellor first ordered a hole cut through the center of the document, all 120 pages of it. Then he ordered that the person who wrote it should have his head stuffed

---

24. *Id.*

25. *Id.* at *2. *See also* Ramos-Barrientos v. Bland, 2008 WL 474426, at *2 (S.D. Ga. Feb. 19, 2008) ("The 'short and plain statement' command is not served by page-long sentences permeated with broken clauses.... Subjects, for that matter, should not have to forage for a verb.").

26. Gordon v. Green, 602 F.2d 743 (5th Cir. 1979).

27. *Id.* at 744. The second heading was a quote from the Bible. *Id.* n.5.

28. *Id.* at 744–45.

29. *Id.* at 745.

30. *Id.* at 746.

31. *Id.*

through the hole, and the unfortunate fellow was led around to be exhibited to all those attending court at West Minister Hall.[32]

Despite getting one more chance, the plaintiff's lawyer could not have been pleased with the court's dim public assessment of his written work.

Appeals have also been dismissed or declared frivolous because of unduly long, unclear briefs or failures to present cogent legal arguments. For example, in *Sambrano v. Mabus*,[33] the Seventh Circuit held that an appeal was frivolous when the appellant's brief was "almost unintelligible."[34] The statement of jurisdiction, for example, was "incoherent."[35] After reading the brief, the court had "no idea whether [the plaintiff] had a good claim against the [defendant]—but we do know that, if she had, [her lawyer] massacred it."[36]

More recently, the Seventh Circuit took the unusual step of issuing an order to show cause why a lawyer should not be sanctioned or otherwise disciplined for court filings that fell "far below the reasonable standards of practice."[37] The offending lawyer submitted a "bizarre appellate brief laden with assertions that have no basis in the record and arguments that have no basis in law."[38] Tallying 86 "interminable" pages, the brief was neither concise nor clear, leading the court to conclude that "[b]ad writing does not normally warrant sanctions, but we draw the line at gibberish."[39] The court directed the clerk to send its opinion to the Illinois Disciplinary Commission for action.[40]

The Missouri Court of Appeals dismissed an appeal for noncompliance with the briefing rules when the appellant's attorney failed to provide a "cogent analysis" and made "no attempt to connect the facts to the law."[41]

---

32. *Id.* at 747 n.13 (quoting Richard C. Wydick, *Plain English for Lawyers*, 66 CALIF. L. REV. 727 (1978)).

33. 663 F.3d 879 (7th Cir. 2011).

34. *Id.* at 881–82.

35. *Id.*

36. *Id.*

37. McCurry v. Kenco Logistics Servs., LLC, 942 F.3d 783, 792 (7th Cir. 2019).

38. *Id.* at 791.

39. *Id.* at 791–92.

40. *Id.* at 792–93.

41. Farr v. State, 665 S.W.3d 394, 400 (Mo. Ct. App. 2023).

D. More Befuddlement (and Belittlement)

The upcoming chapters include more examples of dismissals based on lawyers' inability to live up to rules requiring clear, succinct writing. But the case below shows that even attorneys who survive dismissal may not come away feeling jubilant, because their flawed work product will forever be on parade in a published court opinion. And here, the judge colorfully scolded counsel for *both* sides, saying his piece (and then some) about their inexpert writing and failure to provide sufficient authority:

Bradshaw v. Unity Marine Corp.

147 F. Supp. 2d 668 (S.D. Tex. 2001)

KENT, District Judge.

....

Before proceeding further, the Court notes that this case involves two extremely likable lawyers, who have together delivered some of the most amateurish pleadings ever to cross the hallowed causeway into Galveston, an effort which leads the Court to surmise but one plausible explanation. Both attorneys have obviously entered into a secret pact—complete with hats, handshakes and cryptic words—to draft their pleadings entirely in crayon on the back sides of gravy-stained paper place mats, in the hope that the Court would be so charmed by their child-like efforts that their utter dearth of legal authorities in their briefing would go unnoticed. Whatever actually occurred, the Court is now faced with the daunting task of deciphering their submissions. With [notepad] readied, thick black pencil in hand, and a devil-may-care laugh in the face of death, life on the razor's edge sense of exhilaration, the Court begins.

....

Defendant begins the descent into Alice's Wonderland by submitting a Motion that relies upon only one legal authority. The Motion cites a Fifth Circuit case which stands for the whopping proposition that a federal court sitting in Texas applies the Texas statutes of limitations to certain state and federal law claims. That is all well and good—the Court is quite fond of the *Erie* doctrine; indeed there is talk of little else around both the Canal and this Court's water cooler. Defendant, however, does not even cite to *Erie*, but to a mere successor case, and further fails to even begin to analyze why the Court should approach the shores of *Erie*. Finally, Defendant does not even provide a cite to its desired Texas limitation statute. A more bumbling approach is difficult to conceive—but wait folks, There's More!

Plaintiff responds to this deft, yet minimalist analytical wizardry with an equally gossamer wisp of an argument... [without] any analysis whatsoever of why his claim versus Defendant Phillips is a maritime action. Instead, Plaintiff "cites" to a single case from the Fourth Circuit. Plaintiff's citation, however, points to a nonexistent Volume "1886" of the Federal Reporter Third Edition and neglects to provide a pinpoint citation for what, after being located, turned out to be a forty-page decision.... The Court cannot even begin to comprehend why this case was selected for reference. It is almost as if Plaintiff's counsel chose the opinion by throwing long range darts at the Federal Reporter (remarkably enough hitting a nonexistent volume!). And though the Court often gives great heed to dicta from courts as far flung as those of Manitoba, it finds this case unpersuasive. There is nothing in Plaintiff's cited case about ingress or egress between a vessel and a dock....

Further, as noted above, Plaintiff has submitted a Supplemental Opposition to Defendant's Motion. This Supplement is longer than Plaintiff's purported Response, cites more cases, several constituting binding authority from either the Fifth Circuit or the Supreme Court, and actually includes attachments which purport to be evidence. However, this is all that can be said positively for Plaintiff's Supplement, which does *nothing* to explain why, on the facts of *this* case, Plaintiff has an admiralty claim against Phillips (which probably makes some sense because Plaintiff doesn't).... Despite the continued shortcomings of Plaintiff's supplemental submission, the Court commends Plaintiff for his vastly improved choice of crayon—Brick Red is much easier on the eyes than Goldenrod, and stands out much better amidst the mustard splotched about Plaintiff's briefing. But at the end of the day, even if you put a calico dress on it and call it Florence, a pig is still a pig.

Now, alas, the Court must return to grownup land.

....

After this remarkably long walk on a short legal pier, having received no useful guidance whatever from either party, the Court has endeavored, primarily based upon its affection for both counsel, but also out of its own sense of morbid curiosity, to resolve what it perceived to be the legal issue presented. Despite the waste of perfectly good crayon seen in both parties' briefing (and the inexplicable odor of wet dog emanating from such) the Court believes it has satisfactorily resolved this matter. Defendant's Motion for Summary Judgment is granted.

At this juncture, Plaintiff retains, albeit seemingly to his befuddlement and/or consternation, a maritime law cause of action.... However, it is well known around these parts that Unity Marine's lawyer is equally likable and has been writing crisply in ink since the second grade. Some old-timers even spin yarns of an ability to type. The Court cannot speak to the veracity of such loose talk, but out of caution, the Court suggests that Plaintiff's lovable counsel had best upgrade to a nice shiny No. 2 pencil or at least sharpen what's left of the stubs of his crayons for what remains of this heart-stopping, spine-tingling action.

■ ■ ■

Despite the *Bradshaw* court's caustic feedback, it did not discipline the lawyers. But the cases discussed in the next chapter reveal that courts will indeed sanction lawyers for substandard written work.

E. Funny, but Not: The Takeaway

Will Rogers, an American humorist, actor, and author, famously said this about lawyers and their writing:

> The minute you read something and you can't understand it, you can be sure it was written by a lawyer. Then, if you give it to another lawyer to read and he don't know just what it means, then you can be sure it was drawn up by a lawyer. If it's in a few words and is plain, and understandable only one way, it was written by a non-lawyer.[42]

Funny, yes. But what's less funny is that, as you've seen already, poor legal writing can get lawyers and their clients into hot water. You do not want to be that lawyer, so make the most of your legal-writing courses. Focus on learning how to write clearly, accurately, and concisely. And remember that improper grammar and punctuation—and style missteps—can have disastrous consequences for you, your reputation, and your clients. After all, you don't want to be the lawyer who a federal judge accuses, in a published opinion, of writing court briefs with a crayon.

---

42. Sandy F. Kraemer, *Will Rogers—The Legal Profession's Best Critic*, 59 J. AM. BAR ASS'N 1431, 1431 (Dec. 1973).

Notes and Questions

1. ***Food for Thought***: What do you think of the above cases? Do they surprise you? Why? What do they say about the importance of writing in law practice?
2. ***"Just" Grammar?*** What do the above cases say about a lawyer's need for sound writing mechanics? What about law students? Should your law-school writing courses include instruction or review of basic grammar and punctuation? Why? Why not?
3. ***All Subjective?*** Do you think that the punctuation rules are mostly subjective? If so, try an internet search on punctuation rules and compare what you see on the different websites. Is there consistency?
4. ***Clarity***: Is it possible to write a clear, effective legal document—one that a judge, a client, or a supervisor can easily understand—with poor grammar and punctuation? Can a lawyer impress readers while also making mechanical errors?
5. ***Editorial Polish***: When you read casebooks or other texts for homework, do you ever spot glaring typos or grammatical errors? What if you did? What would you think about the author and the publisher? How would you judge the book's quality and credibility? Should you strive for the same polish in your writing assignments? Why?

TWO

Effective Writing Is Ethical Lawyering

A. Overview

The cases in Chapter 1 focused on writing skill and how subpar writing can impact cases or drag down a lawyer's reputation for style or technical ability. But deficient writing also implicates legal ethics. Lawyers are bound by ethics rules requiring competence and civility.[1] The discussion and cases below explore these sides of a legal writer's professional imperative.

B. Effective Writing as a Professional Responsibility

Ethics are part of every lawyer's professional life, and ethical standards should and arguably do include a duty to write competently.[2] Rule 1.1 of the

---

1. *See* Wendy Muchman, *The Effective Lawyer: Communication, Cultural Competence, and Civility*, AM. BAR. ASS'N (Jan. 20, 2023), https://www.americanbar.org/groups/government_public/publications/public-lawyer/2023-winter/effective-lawyer-communication-cultural-competence-civility/.

2. *E.g.*, Heidi K. Brown, *Breaking Bad Briefs*, 41 J. LEGAL PROF. 259, 295–97 (2017); Debra R. Cohen, *Competent Legal Writing—A Lawyer's Professional Responsibility*, 67 U. CIN. L. REV. 491, 517–19 (1999); Gerald Lebovits, *Legal-Writing Ethics—Part I*, 77 N.Y. ST. B.J. 64 (Oct. 2005); Diana J. Simon, *More True Confessions of a Legal Writing Professor:*

Model Rules of Professional Responsibility provides that a "lawyer shall provide competent representation."[3] "Competent representation" is defined to include, in part, "[s]ome important legal skills, such as the analysis of precedent, the evaluation of evidence and legal drafting."[4] And a lawyer's ethical duty to communicate with—and explain matters to—clients strongly connotes effective written communication.[5] True, the above definition of "competent representation" is somewhat vague because it leaves the precise scope of "drafting" unclear and doesn't explicitly refer to the broader skill of "legal writing." And states generally do not require attorneys to participate in annual continuing legal education devoted exclusively to legal writing.[6] Nonetheless, courts have disciplined lawyers for ineffective legal writing, especially when accompanied by other misconduct. And often state bar associations or ethics committees initiate and pursue those cases.

For example, the Second Circuit upheld a two-year suspension when the Committee on Admissions and Grievances concluded that an attorney filed appellate briefs of "shockingly poor quality."[7] Specifically, the briefs got client names wrong, contained irrelevant boilerplate, and, in some places, were simply unintelligible.[8] As a result, the Committee ordered the lawyer to attend continuing-education programs in brief writing.[9] On appeal, the court was especially disturbed by the attorney's "extremely poor briefing," along with other misconduct, and upheld the two-year suspension.[10] Although the lawyer argued on appeal that he had "submitted a good brief" and showed "much improved writing," the court was not persuaded.[11]

The Continuing Study of Legal Writing Should Be Deemed a Required Part of Our Professional Responsibility, Ariz. Att'y, June 2023.

3. Model Rules of Prof'l Conduct R. 1.1 (Am. Bar Ass'n 1983).

4. *Id.* cmt. 1, https://www.americanbar.org/groups/professional_responsibility/publications/model_rules_of_professional_conduct/rule_1_1_competence/comment_on_rule_1_1/.

5. Muchman, *supra* note 1, at n.42.

6. Brown, *supra* note 2, at 296.

7. In re Sobolevsky, 430 F. App'x 9, 9 (2d Cir. 2011).

8. *Id.* at 17.

9. *Id.* at 22.

10. *Id.* at 10.

11. *Id.*

Similarly, the Utah Supreme Court affirmed a trial court's decision to disbar an attorney based on, among other improper actions, her filing of "often incomprehensible pleadings and memoranda."[12] In fact, one of the many judges forced to read the lawyer's motions stated that "counsel ha[d] taken a dramatically different approach to pleading... claims, at times shuffling each plaintiff's factual allegations and legal assertions together as one would a deck of playing cards, sacrificing narrative sequence in favor of argumentative assertions and conclusory assertions."[13] Other judges commented that her motions were repetitive and "barely comprehensible."[14]

The Kentucky Supreme Court upheld the 60-day suspension of a lawyer whose brief was "little more than fifteen unclear and ungrammatical sentences, slapped together as two pages of unedited text with an unintelligible message."[15] The court added that the brief "would compare unfavorably with the majority of the handwritten pro se pleadings prepared by laypersons which this Court reviews on a daily basis."[16]

And the Vermont Supreme Court ordered that a lawyer be suspended for no less than six months until he could prove that he was fit to practice law.[17] Specifically, the lawyer had earlier agreed to participate in tutoring to develop his skills in persuasive writing, proper organization, and legal analysis, after which he was required to prepare a ten-page writing sample.[18] But he didn't complete the tutorial. The court found that the lawyer had not served his clients adequately because he prepared "inadequate and incomprehensible legal briefs."[19]

---

12. Rose v. Off. of Prof'l Conduct, 424 P.3d 134, 136–38 (Utah 2017).

13. *Id.* at 139.

14. *Id.* at 142.

15. Kentucky Bar Ass'n v. Brown, 14 S.W.3d 916, 918–20 (Ky. 2000) (quoting the Kentucky Bar Association).

16. *Id.* at 919.

17. In re Shepperson, 674 A.2d 1273, 1274–75 (Vt. 1996).

18. *Id.* at 1273–74.

19. *Id.* at 1274–75.

C. Writing Must Meet Professional-Conduct Standards, Too

Besides the need to write competently, lawyers must write with civility and professionalism to meet their ethical responsibilities. Courts have made this point repeatedly. In numerous opinions, judges have admonished lawyers for using sharp language that fails to uphold professional standards.

In a 2023 case, a federal judge observed that "[t]he briefing and...email communications" between opposing counsel "reveal[ed] a breakdown of civility and professionalism."[20] The court noted that it would "not tolerate incivility and lack of professionalism among counsel," reminding the attorneys that their professional obligations included writing with civility:

> [T]he Court reminds counsel of the relevant portions of four professional standards which govern lawyers participating in litigation in this Circuit:...We will treat all other counsel, parties, and witnesses in a civil and courteous manner, not only in court, *but also in all other written...communications*;...We will...*write civilly and respectfully in all communications with the court.*[21]

In 2022, a New York judge admonished an attorney for filing a frivolous motion and for writing emails that disparaged the judiciary and used aggressive language. While the court stopped short of sanctioning the offending attorney, it reminded him that "[w]hether orally or in writing, lawyers should avoid vulgar language, disparaging personal remarks or acrimony toward other counsel, parties or witnesses."[22] In a similar case, in which opposing counsel had exchanged "shrill" letters, the court observed that although the parties' mutual animus may have tempted their attorneys to act in kind, "attorneys are professionals and must resist that tendency."[23]

---

20. Gibbs v. ABT Elecs., Inc., 2023 WL 6809610, at *13 (N.D. Ill. Oct. 16, 2023).

21. *Id.* (quoting Seventh Circuit Standards for Professional Conduct) (emphasis added) (cleaned up).

22. Barrier Assoc. Inc. v. Eagle Eye Adv. LLC, 179 N.Y.S.3d 891, at *15–16 (N.Y. Sup. Ct. 2022) (unreported) (quoting New York State Standards of Civility) (emphasis added) (cleaned up).

23. Topps Co. v. Cadbury Stani S.A.I.C., 2005 WL 2464963, at *4 (S.D.N.Y. Oct. 6, 2005).

The Third Circuit said the same in a case involving personal attacks in a party's appellate briefs. After striking the offending lawyer's first brief, the court later complained that "[t]he new brief [was] not much improved over the original as it continue[d] to make disrespectful, unwarranted allegations" against an administrative-law judge.[24] The court felt "obliged to advise counsel that his lack of professionalism harm[ed] the interest of his client and adversely affect[ed] his credibility."[25]

In short, lawyers who litter their motions, briefs, or pleadings with personal attacks may face a variety of consequences. At best (for offending advocates, that is), courts may simply ignore the attacks.[26] Or courts may take more affirmative steps, such as striking offensive documents in whole or in part[27] or admonishing lawyers to avoid future attacks.[28] Courts may also sanction attorneys.[29] One creative judge who'd had his fill of personal attacks warned the offending attorneys that future attacks would be "sanctioned at $50 per word."[30]

In the following case, an attorney who ignored repeated warnings to avoid personal attacks in his appellate briefs ended up facing more than a lost appeal:

Cruz v. Commissioner of Social Security

244 F. App'x 475 (3d Cir. 2007)

JORDAN, Circuit Judge.

Jose Cruz appeals from an order of the United States District Court for the District of New Jersey affirming the decision of an Administrative Law

24. Meyler v. Comm'r of Soc. Sec., 238 F. App'x 884, 888 n.2 (3d Cir.) (unpublished), *as amended* (Aug. 29, 2007).

25. *Id.*

26. *See, e.g.*, Siemens Transp. P'ship Puerto Rico, S.E. v. Redondo Perini Joint Venture, 2006 WL 2660707, at *6 (N.Y. Sup. Ct. Sept. 15, 2006).

27. *See, e.g.*, Allen v. Ghoulish Gallery, 2008 WL 474394, at *2 (S.D. Cal. Feb. 19, 2008) (striking portions of pleading); *Meyler*, 238 F. App'x at 888 n.2 (striking entire appeal brief).

28. *See, e.g.*, Great Wall Acupuncture, P.C. v. Gen. Assurance Co., 871 N.YS.2d 582, 584 (App. Term 2008); Carstarphen v. Deutsche Bank Nat. Trust Co., 2009 WL 1537861, at *13 n.8 (S.D. Ala. June 1, 2009).

29. Thomas v. Tenneco Packaging Co., 293 F.3d 1306, 1308 (11th Cir. 2002).

30. Wall v. Leavitt, 2007 WL 4219162, at *1 (E.D. Cal. Nov. 29, 2007).

Judge (ALJ) denying his claim for Supplemental Security Income and Disability Insurance Benefits.

....

Because the ALJ examined all of the evidence, made determinations as to the relative credibility of conflicting medical records, and properly supported those determinations by reference to the record, his ruling is supported by substantial evidence. Therefore, we affirm the decision of the District Court.

....

We are required to add a regrettable coda by noting that Cruz's attorney, Mr. Alter, made several unprofessional comments in his brief, going so far as to accuse the ALJ of misconduct. For example, in his discussion of the step-three analysis, he writes that the ALJ "intentionally fixed the analysis to avoid what he knows to be the appropriate listing," "finess[ed] step three," and "tortur[ed] the evidence to death." He also accuses the ALJ of "not be[ing] an objective decider of the facts," "hav[ing] an agenda," making "intentional errors," arriving at a "predictably goal-directed decision," and "wish[ing] diagnoses and restrictions away." Finally he calls the ALJ's decision a "disaster [that] must be sent back from whence it came," and demands that his client be "put out of his social security misery." Heated rhetoric like this does nothing to advance a client's cause. It serves only to distract attention from the merits and to call counsel's judgment into question.

Were this counsel's first offense, this might warrant nothing more than a footnote. But it is not.... His history of unprofessional conduct before us extends back to at least October 2000. In the brief he filed in Frazier v. Commissioner of Social Security, No. 00-1427, 242 F.3d 370 (3d Cir. Oct. 23, 2000), he hurled insults in a manner that has become his trademark. After calling the ALJ's decision "entirely incompetent," 2000 WL 34024365 at *8, he proceeded to discuss the ALJ's "breathtaking ignorance," id. at *11, the ALJ's "ridiculous assumption," id. at *13, and the ALJ's attempted "evidence nullification," id. at *16, and "quackery," id. at *17 n. 1. He summed up by concluding that the ALJ's "analysis is one-third invention, one-third ignorance and one-third inspiration." Id. at *18....

....

This year, Mr. Alter has accelerated the pace of his unprofessional outbursts.... The brief he filed in Meyler v. Commissioner of Social Security was struck for violating Local Appellate Rule 28.1(c), which requires "counsel to exercise appropriate professional behavior in all briefs and to refrain from making ad hominem attacks on opposing counsel or parties." See Docket for Meyler, No. 06-4280 (3d Cir. June 22, 2007). The order striking the brief criticized his work for being "rife with ad hominem attacks," and employing "language that we deem offensive and for which there can be no justification or excuse." Id. We further warned that "any such similar conduct [in the future] will result in the issuance of an Order to Show Cause as to why [Alter] should not be sanctioned under Rules 11(b) and (c) of the Federal Rules of Civil Procedure." Id. . . .

These reprimands, spanning a period of seven years, indicate a serious pattern of unprofessional and offensive behavior. . . . Viewing this steady stream of invective, and at the risk of some heat in our own language, we have concluded that the court can no longer tolerate the pollution of appellate practice that these repeated ad hominem attacks represent. Consequently, we refer Mr. Alter to the Court's Standing Committee on Attorney Discipline so that the Committee may make a recommendation to the Court as to whether Mr. Alter should be disciplined for his repeated violations of Local Rule 28.1(c), his consistent disregard of the many reprimands he has received for those violations, and for conduct unbecoming a member of the bar of this court. See Rule 4.2, Third Circuit Rules of Attorney Disciplinary Enforcement.

Notes and Questions

1. **Cruz *Postscript***: The Third Circuit's Standing Committee on Attorney Discipline later recommended that the court publicly reprimand Cruz's attorney. The court adopted that recommendation, publicly reprimanding the attorney "for his intemperate and inflammatory language in his briefs filed in this Court."[31] The court opted against a more severe penalty—suspension—because of mitigating factors. And the attorney "took full responsibility for his actions and did not attempt to justify them."[32]
2. ***Civility Rules***: Although courts speak of their inherent power to address personal attacks, court rules may also empower courts to act. For instance, Fed. R. Civ. P. 12(f) provides that federal courts may, on their own initiative or on motion, "strike from a plead-

---

31. In re Alter, 264 F. App'x 195, 196 (3d Cir. 2008) (unpublished).

32. *Id.*

ing...any...immaterial, impertinent, or scandalous matter." A federal judge invoked this rule in *Wade v. Smith*, stating that a complaint "riddled with ad hominem attacks" could be struck under Rule 12(f).[33]

3. ***Attacks on Witnesses***: Most cases on this topic involve lawyers' personal attacks on opposing counsel, opposing parties, or judicial officers. But courts seem equally annoyed by personal attacks on adverse witnesses. For example, in *Benedetto v. Commissioner of Social Security*, the Third Circuit expressed its "displeasure" with an appellate attorney whose brief included "repeated ad hominem attacks" on an adverse medical witness.[34]
4. ***Advocacy without Attacks***: Can attorneys be zealous advocates without resorting to personal attacks and inflammatory language? How? What writing techniques make legal arguments forceful and credible without personal attacks?
5. ***Further Reading***: You'll find an informative discussion on writing with civility in Chapter 10 of Judith D. Fischer's excellent book *Pleasing the Court: Writing Ethical and Effective Briefs* (2d ed., Carolina Academic Press 2011).

33. 1991 WL 504873, at *2 (S.D. Ind. May 30, 1991).

34. 2007 WL 4395648, at *2 n.2 (3d Cir. Dec. 14, 2007).

THREE

The Power of Plain (and Hazards of Legalese)

A. Overview

"Legalese" is a pejorative term used to describe stereotypical legal style. It's a style familiar to anybody who has braved a website's Terms & Conditions page: dense, overblown prose that reflects little if any desire to communicate in good faith. Consider, for example, the lease guaranty that one of this book's authors signed to secure a daughter's college apartment:

> In consideration for, and as an inducement to us in making the Lease to Resident, and for other good and valuable consideration, the receipt and sufficiency of which is hereby acknowledged, you, as Guarantor, guarantee irrevocably, absolutely and unconditionally, to us and our successors and assigns, the full performance and prompt observance of all the agreements and conditions of the Lease and of any amendments, revisions or renewals of the Lease (and all documents that are a part of the Lease), including, but not limited to, the payment of Rent and other sums due under the Lease. You acknowledge that you have a relationship with the Resident and as a result of that relationship you will derive a substantial benefit from the making of the Lease to Resident. Once you sign this Guaranty it is

your legal obligation to pay us sums due under the Lease. You hereby waive any legal defenses to this Guaranty based on notice of acceptance, presentment, demand, notice of protest, notice of dishonor or default, and notice of any changes, renewals or modifications. Unless we are seeking money from you for your payment responsibilities under this Guaranty, we do not have to provide any notices to you. You hereby waive each and every notice to which you or the Resident might be entitled to under the Lease, or otherwise, including, without limitation, notice of any breach of default by you or the Resident. Once any sums are due under the Lease we may collect them from you without making efforts to sue or otherwise try to collect such sums from the Resident. This is a guaranty of payment and performance and not of collection and your liability is primary and not secondary. You expressly waive any defenses based upon any applicable statute of limitations, failure of us to enforce the Lease against the Resident, any failure to give notice of default to the Resident or other notices due under the Lease and any duty to give you notice of facts about the Resident. We may, on one or more occasions, in our sole discretion, waive terms of the Lease, grant concessions or other indulgences to the Resident all without any notice to you or effect on your obligations to us. As used in this Guaranty, the term "you" shall also include all other persons claiming by, through or under you, including your heirs or personal representatives. You may not assign your obligations under this Guaranty to anyone else. Your liability under this Guaranty continues in full force and effect even if the Resident becomes incapacitated, disabled or bankrupt. You are not released from your guarantee obligations until we have been fully paid all sums due under the Lease. If we institute any legal proceedings against you to enforce this Guaranty and prevail in such action, you will be liable for the costs and expenses of such action incurred by us, including our reasonable attorneys' fees, in addition to any amounts awarded to us in such action. You consent to the jurisdiction of, and venue in, any local or state court otherwise having subject matter jurisdiction and located within __________ County in the State of __________. Your signature below confirms that you have had the opportunity to read and understand this Guaranty and to consult legal counsel if you so desire.

Laypersons aren't alone in recoiling from passages like this.[1] Judges have described legalese as "tortured,"[2] "painful,"[3] "incomprehensible,"[4] "abstruse,"[5] "opaque,"[6] and "mind-numbing."[7] U.S. Supreme Court justices have called legalese "pretentious,"[8] "pointless,"[9] and "Terrible! Terrible!"[10] Justice Ruth Bader Ginsberg "c[ouldn't] bear it."[11] A survey of California appellate judges revealed that "[l]awyers who write in legalese are likely to have their work judged as unpersuasive and substantively weak"—and risk having their "professional credentials...judged as less credible."[12]

So if you embrace legalese after graduation, don't be surprised if you submit a proposed order but the judge edits out the legalese before signing it.[13] Don't be surprised if a judge trying to describe your case relies on your opponent's brief instead of your complaint because the brief "actually makes the facts clearer than does the complaint itself, which is drafted mostly in dense

---

1. *See, e.g.*, N.H. Ball Bearings, Inc. v. Jackson, 969 A.2d 351, 362 (N.H. 2009) ("[L]egalese, at times, can obfuscate the underlying substance and meaning of words."); Sanders v. Ashland Oil, Inc., 696 So. 2d 1031, 1038 (La. App. 1997) ("[W]e note that the agreement is poorly drafted and that the use of legalese, such as 'aforesaid,' makes the meaning of the contract terms unclear.").

2. Weigner v. City of New York, 852 F.2d 646, 656 (2d Cir. 1988).

3. Johnson v. Revenue Mgmt. Corp., 169 F.3d 1057, 1061 (7th Cir. 1999).

4. Marrakush Soc'y v. N.J. St. Police, 2009 WL 2366132, at *12 (D.N.J. July 30, 2009).

5. *Weigner*, 852 F.2d at 656.

6. Canas v. City of Sunnyvale, 2009 WL 2160572, at *5 (N.D. Cal. July 20, 2009).

7. Lorenz v. CSX Corp., 736 F. Supp. 650, 656 (W.D. Pa. 1990).

8. Bryan Garner, Interview with Justice Anthony M. Kennedy, 13 Scribes J. Legal Writing 79, 98 (2010).

9. Bryan Garner, Interview with Justice Stephen G. Breyer, 13 Scribes J. Legal Writing 145, 156 (2010).

10. *Id.*

11. Bryan Garner, Interview with Justice Ruth Bader Ginsburg, 13 Scribes J. Legal Writing 133, 141 (2010).

12. Robert W. Benson & Joan B. Kessler, *Legalese v. Plain English: An Empirical Study of Persuasion and Credibility in Appellate Brief Writing*, 20 Loy. L.A. L. Rev. 301, 319 (1987).

13. *See, e.g.*, Bank of Am. v. Washington, 2009 WL 3229322, at *1 n.1 (M.D. Ga. Oct. 1, 2009) ("Plaintiff's counsel and Defendant HUD's counsel submitted a proposed order containing excessive legalese. The Court has revised the form of that order so that it is more understandable.").

legalese."[14] Don't be surprised if a judge allows you to amend a pleading but instructs you to drop the legalese in the amended version.[15] And don't be surprised if a judge sanctions you for frustrating discovery with legalese-infused objections[16]—or denies your motion to compel discovery because instead of drafting simple and direct requests, you made "overzealous use of legalese."[17]

Yet despite the cautionary evidence, each generation of lawyers seems to perpetuate the legalese legacy, presumably for fear of not fitting in or of making editorial changes with substantive ramifications. Or maybe they've never made the effort to become skilled writers. Whatever the reason, the typical justification is that legal writing "has to be this way" to effectively capture specialized, sophisticated concepts.

But does it?

A recent study in the *International Journal of Cognitive Science* debunks that well-worn claim. The study's authors (scholars at MIT and the University of Edinburgh) found that traditional legal documents are impenetrable not because of sophisticated concepts, but because of "poor writing."[18] The documents they studied were weighed down by, among other things, jargon, passive voice, nonstandard capitalization, and center-embedding.[19] (Center-embedding means inserting complex definitions in the middle of sentences.[20])

And the claim that legalese is somehow necessary was "undercut by [the study's] results and previous findings that show comprehension of legal content with a simplified register."[21] While some terms of art might be inevitable,

---

14. Pinebrook Minerals, LLC v. Anadarko E & P Co., LP, 2011 WL 3584783, at *1 (M.D. Pa. July 25), *report and recommendation adopted*, 2011 WL 3584784 (M.D. Pa. Aug. 15, 2011).

15. *See, e.g.*, *Canas*, 2009 WL 2160572, at *5 ("[P]laintiffs' complaint suffers from multiple defects, including its frequent recourse to opaque and formulaic legalese and its lack of structure.... Plaintiffs are urged to address these defects in any amended pleading....").

16. *See, e.g.*, Trafton v. Rocketplane Kistler, Inc., 2009 WL 2251288, at *1 (E.D. Wis. July 22, 2009) (awarding the plaintiffs $2,500 in legal fees for time spent "trying to make sense of" the defendants' supplemental interrogatory responses, which "continue[d] to obfuscate matters by virtue of their multiple objections and their vexatiously legalese tone").

17. Williams v. Adams, 2009 WL 1220311, at *12 (E.D. Cal. May 1, 2009).

18. Eric Martinez et al., *Poor Writing, Not Specialized Concepts, Drives Processing Difficulty in Legal Language*, 224 COGNITION 1, 1 (July 2022).

19. *Id.* at 1–2.

20. *Id.* at 1.

21. *Id.* at 6.

the study's findings "suggest that in many instances such jargon can be replaced with simpler alternatives that increase recall and comprehension while preserving meaning."[22]

Lawyers who defend traditional style grossly overstate the prevalence of true terms of art. One study found that court-interpreted terms accounted for fewer than 3% of the words in a typical real-estate sales contract.[23] So why such inflated diction and density in the other 97%? Client-conscious lawyers won't tolerate these extra layers of complexity: the advantages (including financial advantages) of clear, reader-centered documents are well documented.[24] This is true in both the business and government sectors.[25]

And lawyers who think that they're playing it safe by recycling dense forms should beware: their safety net has a hole in it. As you'll see in the cases below, the reality is that legalese makes documents *more*, not less, vulnerable to attack. It gives courts a ready-made reason to invalidate provisions that seem one-sided or harsh.

B. In Premarital Agreements

If tempted to adopt a jargon-heavy legal form, consider one husband's futile attempt to enforce a premarital agreement. To enforce it, the husband had to prove that his wife signed it (1) voluntarily, (2) with knowledge of its content and legal effect, and (3) without duress. An appellate court found that the husband proved two of the three: his wife had signed the agreement voluntarily and without duress. So the agreement's enforceability hinged on whether she signed it with knowledge of its content and legal effect. The court's decision focused, in large part, on the unrepresented wife's inability to understand the document's legalese:

---

22. *Id.*

23. Benson Barr et al., *Legalese and the Myth of Case Precedent*, 64 MICH. B.J. 1136, 1137 (Oct. 1985).

24. *See* JOSEPH KIMBLE, WRITING FOR DOLLARS, WRITING TO PLEASE: THE CASE FOR PLAIN LANGUAGE IN BUSINESS, GOVERNMENT, AND LAW Part 5 (Carolina Academic Press 2012).

25. *Id.*

Gochenour v. Gochenour

2023 WL 152171 (W. Va. Ct. App. Jan. 10, 2023)

....

[Before] the parties' marriage, husband owned a motorcycle racing business and had approximately $1,900,000 in assets. Wife had no assets and approximately $18,000 debt.... [T]hirteen days before the wedding, husband presented an ante-nuptial agreement to wife, which was prepared by husband's attorney, and told wife that he would not marry her unless she signed it.

Husband presented testimony in family court that the parties discussed the ante-nuptial agreement several times throughout the relationship and wife was agreeable with it. However, wife testified that the agreement was never brought up until thirteen days before the wedding. Wife further testified that she was upset and did not understand the legalese in the agreement; because she did not understand the legal wording, she only skimmed the agreement. When asked in family court whether she knew the purpose of the agreement, wife stated, "so that I could not take his business." Nonetheless, wife filled out her portion of the agreement and signed before a notary. Wife did not obtain independent counsel and was not verbally instructed to do so.

The parties were married as planned.... Husband continued to grow his business and earned approximately $200,000 per year. Wife completed her teaching degree shortly after the parties married and earned approximately $50,000 per year.... Wife filed for divorce in October of 2021 and husband sought to enforce the ante-nuptial agreement. The ante-nuptial agreement, if valid, would prevent wife from claiming equitable distribution or survivor rights of any kind.

The family court determined that the ante-nuptial agreement was unenforceable and invalid because husband failed to prove the agreement was signed by wife voluntarily, with knowledge of its content and legal effect, and free from duress.... Husband now appeals the family court's ruling....

Wife argues that the agreement was prepared by husband's attorney, with no cover letter, nor any other communication advising her to seek independent counsel. Both parties testified that neither of them discussed the terms of the agreement, nor did they understand them.... With regard to wife having knowledge of the agreement's content and legal effect, she testified that she skimmed the agreement because she did not understand it. Further, husband's attorney did not advise her to seek independent counsel....

After review of the record, the facts demonstrate that husband failed to meet his burden of proving that wife signed the ante-nuptial agreement with knowledge of its content and legal effect. Husband's attorney drafted the agreement and did not encourage wife to seek independent counsel. Both parties testified that they did not understand the legalese within the agreement. The family court found wife's testimony to be credible.

[B]ecause husband failed to prove the agreement was signed with knowledge of its content and legal effect, we conclude the family court did not abuse its discretion when finding that the ante-nuptial agreement is unenforceable.

Accordingly, we affirm.

Notes and Questions

1. ***A Concurring Opinion***: *Gochenour* isn't unique. A Massachusetts court likewise refused to enforce a premarital agreement that the parties could not easily understand:

   > [A]s there is no express waiver of marital rights in the agreement, nor plain language or other evidence demonstrating that the parties sufficiently understood their marital rights and how they were altering them, and as the contesting party was not represented by legal counsel or even advised to seek such counsel, we conclude that the agreement does not contain a proper waiver of marital rights and is therefore invalid.[26]

2. ***Reflection***: Might the outcome have been different in *Gochenour* and *Eyster* had the attorneys drafted the agreements in a plain style, perhaps with informative question-style headings that are becoming common in consumer documents?
3. ***Consumer Documents***: Is legalese self-defeating for any type of consumer document? Consider *Tenney v. Deutsche Bank Trust Corp.*, in which the court refused to enforce a bank's "Certificate of Confirmation of Notice of Right to Rescind," which was "drafted in legalese that [was] unnecessarily convoluted and difficult for the

26. Eyster v. Pechenik, 887 N.E.2d 272, 283 (Mass. Ct. App. 2008).

average consumer to read."[27] Given the legalese and other shortcomings, the court held that the certificate violated the Truth in Lending Act because it "would confuse and mislead the average consumer."[28]

C. In Pre-injury Releases

Legalese can also doom exculpatory releases designed to avoid personal-injury suits. In some jurisdictions, these releases are disfavored to begin with.[29] So courts seem to be on the lookout for any and every reason to invalidate them, whether it's overbreadth,[30] internal inconsistency,[31] confusion from redundancy,[32] or some other flaw. Adding layers of legalese only invites harsher scrutiny. Consider a case in which the court declined to enforce a health club's release, noting, among other things, that it was "replete with legal jargon":

Stone v. Life Time Fitness, Inc.

411 P.3d 225 (Colo. Ct. App. 1st Div. 2016),
modified (Jan. 12, 2017)

....

The validity of exculpatory clauses releasing or waiving future negligence claims usually turns on the fourth *Jones* factor—whether the intention of the parties is expressed in clear and unambiguous language.... This case also turns on that factor.

....

---

27. 2009 WL 415510, at *4 (D. Mass. Jan. 26, 2009).

28. *Id.* at *5.

29. *See, e.g.*, Cunningham v. Weber Cnty., 506 P.3d 575, 578 (Utah 2022) ("Utah law disfavors preinjury releases.").

30. *See, e.g.*, *id.* at 580.

31. *See, e.g.*, dōTERRA Int'l, LLC v. Kruger, 491 P.3d 939, 945 (Utah 2021) (refusing to enforce release that sought to avoid "any and all liability" but elsewhere listed damages without any reference to liability for personal injury); Fresnedo v. Porky's Gym III, Inc., 271 So. 3d 1185, 1187–89 (Fla. Dist. Ct. App. 2019) (refusing to enforce health club's release when the clear meaning of a fourth provision was clouded by similar language in the first two provisions).

32. *See, e.g.*, *Fresnedo*, 271 So. 3d at 1187–89.

We conclude that the Agreement fails this test for numerous reasons.

First, as explained by the New York Court of Appeals, "a provision that would exempt its drafter from any liability occasioned by his fault should not compel resort to a magnifying glass and lexicon." . . . Here, the Agreement consists of extremely dense fine print, for which a great many people would require a magnifying glass or magnifying reading glasses.

Second, the two clauses are replete with legal jargon, using phrases and terms such as "affiliates, subsidiaries, successors, or assigns"; "assumption of risk"; "inherent risk of injury"; "includes, but is not limited to"; and "I agree to defend, indemnify and hold Life Time Fitness harmless." The use of such technical legal language militates against the conclusion that the release of liability was clear and simple to a lay person.

Third, the first of the two clauses relied on by Life Time bears the following heading: "under Chapter 458, 459, 460, or Chapter 461 ASSUMPTION OF RISK." At oral argument, counsel for Life Time conceded that the reference to multiple chapters was ambiguous and confusing, and he could not explain to what the chapters referred. Our research has not enlightened us on the subject. Conscientious lay persons could reasonably have skipped over the fine print appearing under that heading, believing it did not apply to them because they would have no reason to understand that chapters 458, 459, 460, or 461 had any relevance to their situation. Thus, the assumption of risk heading was not clear and unambiguous.

Fourth, the dominant focus of the Agreement is on the risks of strenuous exercise and use of exercise equipment at the fitness center[,] [but the plaintiff's injuries arose from tripping on a cord in the locker room.]

Fifth, the term "inherent risk of injury" that appears in the assumption of risk clause has been applied in various Colorado statutes and case law to address waivers of liability only for activities that are dangerous or potentially dangerous. . . . Significantly, not one of these statutory exemptions from liability extends to the use of locker rooms, rest rooms, or dressing rooms associated with these activities. Rather, the releases of liability extend only to the dangerous or potentially dangerous activities themselves.

. . . .

In light of this statutory and case law backdrop, the use of the inherent risk language in the assumption of risk clause, and the Agreement's focus on the use of exercise equipment and facilities and physical injuries resulting from strenuous exercise, one could reasonably conclude that by signing the Agreement he or she was waiving claims based only on the inherent risks of injury related to fitness activities, as opposed to washing one's hands. Indeed,

Stone so stated in her affidavit submitted in opposition to the motion for summary judgment.

Sixth, Life Time contends that the only relevant language we need consider is that set forth in the second exculpatory clause, labeled "RELEASE OF LIABILITY." That provision begins by stating that "I waive any and all claims or actions that may arise against Life Time...as a result of any *such* injury." (Emphasis added.) The quoted language, however, is the first use of the term "injury" in the release of liability clause. So the scope of the release can be determined only by referring back to the confusing assumption of risk clause. It is not surprising then that Life Time's counsel characterized the release's reference to "such injury" as "squirrely." In any event, all of the ambiguities and confusion in the assumption of risk clause necessarily infect the release clause.

Seventh, the exculpatory clauses repeatedly use the phrases "includes, but is not limited to" and "including and without limitation," as well as simply "including." The repeated use of these phrases makes the clauses more confusing, and the reader is left to guess whether the phrases have different meanings. The problem is compounded by conflicting views expressed by divisions of this court on whether the similar phrase "including, but not limited to" is expansive or restrictive....For purposes of deciding this case we need not resolve this conflict; the relevance of the conflict for present purposes is that it creates another ambiguity.

That ambiguity—expansive versus restrictive—is critical because nothing in the Agreement refers to risks of using sinks or locker rooms. The assumption of risk clause refers to the "risk of loss, theft or damage of personal property" for the member or her guests while "using any lockers" at a Life Time fitness center. That is quite a separate matter, however, from suffering a physical injury in a locker room.

....

Based on the foregoing discussion, and after scrutinizing the exculpatory clauses, we conclude that the Agreement uses excessive legal jargon, is unnecessarily complex, and creates a likelihood of confusion or failure of a party to recognize the full extent of the release provisions....Accordingly, the Agreement does not clearly, unambiguously, and unequivocally bar Stone's PLA claim based on the injuries she alleges she sustained after she washed her hands in the women's locker room.

Notes and Questions

1. ***A Concurring Opinion***: In the 2022 Utah Supreme Court case *Cunningham v. Weber County*, the court likewise refused to enforce a pre-injury release because its meaning was not clear and unmistakable:

   > [A] preinjury release must clearly and unmistakably inform a reasonable person who *and* what she is releasing to be enforceable. It is not enough that we might be able to squint at the preinjury release language and conclude that a reader "might have known" or "probably knew" that she was releasing a certain party or claim.
   >
   > ....
   >
   > Simply stated, the preinjury release Cunningham signed was not clear and unmistakable. It was therefore unenforceable, and the district court erred when it concluded otherwise and granted summary judgment.[33]

2. ***A Plain Version***: Professor Joseph Kimble, who has edited the *Michigan Bar Journal*'s "Plain Language" column for more than 30 years, published his redraft[34] of a city's release form:

33. 506 P.3d 575, 580 (Utah 2022).

34. Joseph Kimble, *Cleaning Up a Release*, 87 MICH. B.J. 38, 39 (Mar. 2008).

Release of Legal Claims

What I'm giving up

If I suffer any injury or damages from participating in the Capital City "Clean Sweep," I release, or give up, any legal claim that I might have against the following for their negligent conduct:

- The City of Lansing.
- My employer.
- A sponsoring organization.
- Any of their officers, employees, agents, or volunteers.

This release is binding on my legal representatives or anyone who tries to claim through me.

[*If the sponsor really wants an indemnity provision, which seems rather unreasonable . . .*

What I'm agreeing to pay for

If anyone listed above (in the four bullet points) is sued or has to pay anyone else because of my conduct, I will reimburse them for their legal costs, fees, and payments.]

My health; permission to get medical help

I don't know of any health condition of mine that could get worse if I participate in the Clean Sweep. I authorize the City of Lansing's staff to get emergency medical treatment for me during the Clean Sweep.

My understanding of this release

I have read this release, I understand it, and I sign it freely.

Do you think that a judge would be reluctant to enforce Professor Kimble's document? Would a party who signed it have grounds to argue that they didn't understand it? Do the cases discussed in this chapter support your conclusion?

D. In Indemnity Clauses

Even in cases with a commercial flavor, courts' concerns over legalese may be heightened if laypeople might read the document. Consider a Maryland case involving an indemnification dispute between two business entities. In refusing to enforce a property-management company's form contract, the court expressed concern for lay homeowners who might be asked to sign it:

Twarowski v. Heart's Desire DCL

2021 WL 5359668 (D. Md. Nov. 17, 2021)

STEPHANIE A. GALLAGHER, United States District Judge

. . . .

The operative question, then, is whether the indemnification clause, as drafted, is enforceable under Maryland law if Taylor-Made is found liable for the Plaintiffs' injuries.

In Maryland, indemnification clauses seeking to indemnify a party for its own negligence are presumed to be unenforceable, unless the language expressly and plainly explains the clause's effect. The Court of Appeals explained, "[A]n indemnity contract will be strictly construed against the indemnitees and will not be construed as indemnifying one against his own negligence unless such a construction is required by clear and explicit language of the contract." In a 2015 case, the Court of Appeals reiterated that the presumption against an indemnification agreement covering liability resulting from the indemnitee's own negligence applies "unless an intention to [cover such liability] is expressed in those very words or in other unequivocal terms."

The indemnification clause in this case does not clearly and unequivocally state that the Owner will indemnify Taylor-Made for its own negligence. Instead, in relatively convoluted legalese, it provides for broad indemnification "except as such may be the result of Agent's gross negligence or willful and intentional misconduct." Given that the PMA is a form contract drafted by Taylor-Made, apparently intended for signature by individual homeowners who may or may not be legally savvy, the indemnification clause does not contain the explicit language Maryland law requires to permit a party to enjoy indemnification for its own negligent conduct. Inclusion of the reference to "gross negligence or willful and intentional misconduct" may be significant to an attorney or legal scholar, but would not clearly indicate to a layperson that the layperson is agreeing to be liable for Taylor-Made's negligent acts.

Accordingly, summary judgment as to Count Two in favor of Heart's Desire is also warranted, because the indemnification clause as drafted is not enforceable under Maryland law.

Notes and Questions

1. ***Notice Requires Clarity***: Dense legalese prompted the Eighth Circuit to hold that an airline employee's civil claim against his employer was not discharged in the airline's bankruptcy case. The court reasoned that the airline's notice of the deadline for submitting prepetition claims was too confusing. The notice's language, the court explained, would have taxed even an attorney's ability to understand that the deadline applied to the employee's claim:

   > The district court characterized the notice, we think fairly, as "dense with legalese." Our ruling today confirms that, even if Sanchez consulted an attorney concerning the scope of this notice (and it is not a foregone conclusion he was expected to do so...), an attorney would be justified in advising Sanchez not to file a request for payment of an administrative expense because his claim fell within one of the five exceptions. Under these circumstances, Sanchez did not receive a notice fairly apprising him of the possibility his claim would be discharged if not submitted by the bar date. *See Fogel v. Zell*, 221 F.3d 955, 962 (7th Cir. 2000) ("If the notice is unclear, the fact that it was received will not make it adequate.").... [W]e thus conclude Sanchez's claim under the ADA was not discharged in Northwest's bankruptcy.

2. ***Bias from Legalese?*** A federal court "adjusted" a class-action notice after the defendant objected that its legalese violated Fed. R. Civ. P. 23's requirement that notices be written "clearly and concisely" and "in plain, easily understood language." The defendant was concerned that having its defenses described in legalese would create bias against it:

   > Fourth, where the Notice does address defenses, Defendant asserts the legalese creates bias and fails to be clear and concise as required by the Federal Rules....

> The Court has adjusted the Notice where legalese obscures the clarity of the Notice.

3. ***RICO Scheme***: In finding that investors had stated a claim for racketeering, a California court noted that the defendants who'd allegedly defrauded the investors provided "prospectuses containing thousands of pages of dense and complicated legalese." The defendants had then told brokers "to disregard the prospectuses and rely upon fact sheets" that failed to disclose the investments' high risk levels.[35]
4. ***Invalid Arbitration Award***: "Nonsense legalese" in a purported arbitration award, among other things, helped a federal judge sniff out a fraudulent arbitration scheme:

> The document never states details of the "contract" in any concrete terms.... The whole of the 22-page document, drafted with repetitive, nonsense legalese, contains no factual or legal conclusions from which this Court could deduce the existence of a valid contract, let alone a valid agreement to arbitrate.
>
> ....
>
> [A]s the Court finds that the arbitration documents have no legal validity, the award must be vacated.... Plaintiffs have failed to demonstrate the existence of a valid agreement to arbitrate with any of the Defendants, rendering the arbitration proceedings and associated award meritless.

E. The Plain Difference

On the flip side, courts have cited the absence of legalese as a reason to enforce legal documents.[36] For instance, the Tenth Circuit enforced an indemnification clause that was "clear and unambiguous" and "written in plain language, not hidden nor lost in a haze of small print and legalese." The clause was also "conspicuously labeled and easily identified." A district court likewise

---

35. *Id.*

36. *See, e.g.*, Smith v. Amedisys, Inc., 298 F.3d 434, 444 (5th Cir. 2002) (upholding a preinjury release).

upheld a severability clause that "d[id] not contain any fine print, confusing legalese, and appear[ed] to have been printed in twelve or thirteen point font."[37] And another federal judge rejected a party's claim that it hadn't received reasonable notice of a contract provision when the relevant language was "clear and easily understood" and was not "buried in pages of fine print and legalese."

The outcome was the same in the following case, in which a brokerage firm successfully relied on a clearly written clause that withheld payouts to ex-spouses who'd been named as beneficiaries before divorcing the account holder:

Hartley-Bartman v. Merrill Lynch, Pierce, Fenner & Smith, Inc.

2021 WL 4841136 (Md. Ct. Spec. App. Oct. 18, 2021)

. . . .

We initially note that appellant does not claim that the Re-designation Provision is ambiguous. Instead, she argues that the Re-designation Provision is unenforceable because it is unconscionable. To be void and unenforceable, a contract provision must be both procedurally and substantively unconscionable.

. . . .

The Re-designation Provision is not, as appellant appears to argue, inconspicuously hidden within dozens of pages of fine print. On the whole, the contract documents are presented in a format that is easy to read, and the contractual language is not littered with overly complicated sentences or unnecessary "legalese." The Re-designation Provision appears twice in the contract documents—once in the Traditional IRA Disclosure Statement and once in the Traditional IRA Custodial Agreement. Both of these documents have clear, easily comprehensible tables of contents spanning only a single page.

In the Disclosure Statement, the Re-designation Provision is found under a main heading titled "DESIGNATING BENEFICIARIES," which has only four sub-categories. The sub-category containing the Re-designation Provision is titled "Changes in family status affecting designations," and is found on page four.

In the Custodial Agreement, the Re-designation Provision is found under a main heading titled "INFORMATION YOU PROVIDE," which has five sub-categories. The category containing the Re-designation Provision is titled

37. Cox v. Station Casinos, LLC, 2014 WL 3747605, at *4 (D. Nev. June 25), *report and recommendation adopted*, 2014 WL 3778241 (D. Nev. July 21, 2014).

"Spousal beneficiaries after divorce or annulment," located three pages after the table of contents.

We reject appellant's assertion that the Re-designation Provision is not "conspicuously distinct," and conclude that the operative agreements are not procedurally unconscionable.[38]

Notes and Questions

1. ***Founders' Frustrations***: Experts have criticized legalese since our nation's founding. John Adams complained about the many "useless words" found in English laws.[39] Thomas Jefferson complained about the "verbosity," the "endless tautologies," and the "multiplied efforts at certainty by *saids* and *aforesaids*."[40] Jefferson believed that this excess made legal writing "more perplexed and incomprehensible, not only to common readers, but to lawyers themselves."[41] Naturally, with this criticism came a need to describe the other end of the spectrum—to label the brand of legal writing that would rise above the pomp. Adams used the phrase "common language."[42] Jefferson talked about "more plain" meaning.[43] It took about two centuries, but "plain" won the day, emerging in the 1970s as the choice adjective for describing a more direct, clear style.[44]
2. ***Follow the Feds***: The federal government has long been a leader in the plain-English movement. In the late 1970s, the Federal Communications Commission rewrote some of its regulations to replace confusing legalese with plain English.[45] In 1998, the Securities and

38. We've added the new paragraph indents to enhance readability.

39. John Adams, *Letter of Sept. 10, 1818, from John Adams to William Tudor, in* 10 The Works of John Adams (Letters 1811–1825) 352 (Little, Brown & Co. 1856) (italics in original).

40. 1 Thomas Jefferson, Autobiography of Thomas Jefferson (1743–1790) 70 (G.P. Putnam's Sons 1914).

41. *Id.*

42. *Id.*

43. *Id.*

44. *Id.*

45. *See* JOSEPH KIMBLE, WRITING FOR DOLLARS, WRITING TO PLEASE: THE CASE FOR PLAIN LANGUAGE IN BUSINESS, GOVERNMENT, AND LAW 107–08 (Carolina Academic Press 2012).

Exchange Commission adopted *A Plain English Handbook—How to Create Clear SEC Disclosure Documents*.[46] In 2003, the Federal Aviation Administration issued Order 1000.36, which adopted writing standards designed to "communicate clearly... and in plain language" rather than with "dense and needlessly complex" language.[47] Other agencies have taken similar steps.[48] And in 2010, Congress enacted the most groundbreaking plain-language directive to date: the Plain Writing Act of 2010. The Act requires federal agencies to use "plain writing" in their documents, meaning "writing that is clear, concise, [and] well-organized, and follows other best practices appropriate to the subject or field and intended audience."[49]

3. ***Resources for the New Editor***: A number of outstanding reference books are available to help you develop your editorial skills. Among the best are:

   - Bryan A. Garner, *The Redbook: A Manual on Legal Style* (any edition)
   - Joseph Kimble, *Lifting the Fog of Legalese: Essays on Plain Language* and *Seeing Through Legalese: More Essays on Plain Language*
   - Megan McAlpin, *Beyond the First Draft: Editing Strategies for Powerful Legal Writing*
   - Richard C. Wydick & Amy E. Sloan, *Plain English for Lawyers* (any edition)

46. Available at https://www.sec.gov/pdf/handbook.pdf.

47. Foreword to FAA Writing Standards, FAA Order No. 1000.36, at 1 (U.S. DOT, FAA Mar. 31, 2003), https://www.faa.gov/documentlibrary/media/order/branding_writing/order1000_36.pdf.

48. See KIMBLE, *supra* note 52, at 80, 108–12 (describing U.S. Department of Veterans Affairs form-letters project).

49. Plain Writing Act of 2010, Pub. L. No. 111-274, §3, 124 Stat. 2861, 2861 (2010); for the story behind the Act, see Annetta Cheek, *The Plain Writing Act of 2010: Getting Democracy to Work for You*, 90 MICH. B.J. 52 (Oct. 2011).

F. AI-Generated Documents

You'll hear the same message from most every legal-writing expert, whether a practitioner or an academic: AI-generated documents mark the beginning of the lawyering process, not the end. For all the hoopla over AI technology, using it to produce legal documents has a familiar feel to any practicing lawyer. Lawyers have always relied on preexisting drafts—sometimes created by predecessors—to get the ball rolling.

So whether creating a first draft with ChatGPT or with a document from a law firm's form/brief bank, lawyers must make that draft their own—substantively, linguistically, and typographically. They must update, modify, rearrange, and check for substantive inaccuracies or omissions. Depending on the document type, they must strive to create cohesion, enhance points of emphasis, and more.

But our overriding message here isn't cautionary. There is much positive potential in artificial intelligence. Just a few tries at drafting contracts with AI software reveals its tremendous capacity to help lawyers work more efficiently and, with careful use, produce first drafts that are more accessible than typical forms.

For example, this book's authors used the most basic version of ChatGPT to redraft the daunting lease guaranty that opened this chapter. Our first instruction to ChatGPT was to "please redraft this contract clause so that it is better organized and uses plain language." ChatGPT's initial redraft greatly improved the original. But it was still fairly dense, so we asked ChatGPT to "please add informative headings." Below is what it produced, without any edits (other than our bolding of the title and headings).

This AI-generated redraft still needs a lot of work. There are vestiges of legalese throughout, despite our request for plain language. For instance, lay readers would surely wonder about the meaning of "good and valuable consideration" and "subject matter jurisdiction." They'd wonder about most of the "Waiver of Legal Defenses" clause. And some of the waiver clauses should probably be merged. The redraft also needs better typography. Still, what you see below is much more approachable than what you saw at the chapter's start:

Guaranty of Lease Agreement

Consideration and Inducement

In consideration for making the Lease to Resident and for other good and valuable consideration, you, as Guarantor, guarantee the full performance and prompt observance of all the agreements and conditions of the Lease.

Guarantor's Relationship with Resident

As Guarantor, you acknowledge that you have a relationship with the Resident and will derive a substantial benefit from the making of the Lease to Resident.

Guarantor's Obligations

Once you sign this Guaranty, you are legally obligated to pay sums due under the Lease. Your liability is primary, and you may not assign your obligations under this Guaranty to anyone else.

Waiver of Legal Defenses

By signing this Guaranty, you waive your right to any legal defenses based on notice of acceptance, presentment, demand, notice of protest, notice of dishonor or default, and notice of any changes, renewals, or modifications.

Waiver of Notices

You waive your right to any notices regarding the Resident's breach of the Lease or any other notices you or the Resident may be entitled to.

Collection from Guarantor

We can collect sums due under the Lease from you without trying to collect from the Resident first.

Waiver of Defenses

You expressly waive any defenses based upon any applicable statute of limitations, failure of us to enforce the Lease against the Resident, any failure to give notice of default to the Resident or other notices due under the Lease, and any duty to give you notice of facts about the Resident.

Waiver of Concessions to Resident

We may waive terms of the Lease, grant concessions or other indulgences to the Resident, all without any notice to you or effect on your obligations to us.

Continuing Liability

Your liability under this Guaranty continues even if the Resident becomes incapacitated, disabled, or bankrupt.

Legal Proceedings

If we need to take legal action to enforce this Guaranty and we prevail, you will be responsible for the costs and expenses incurred by us, including reasonable attorneys' fees.

Consent to Jurisdiction and Venue

You consent to the jurisdiction and venue of any local or state court with subject matter jurisdiction and located within Washtenaw County in the State of Michigan.

Confirmation of Understanding

By signing below, you confirm that you have read and understood this Guaranty and have had the opportunity to consult with legal counsel if you so desire.

G. Exercises

Below are excerpts from actual legal documents. Edit them to enhance readability and clarity. Where appropriate, consider using informative headings and subheadings to aid reader navigation. As you edit, be on the lookout for:

- general wordiness (*due to the fact that* instead of *because*; *for the reason that* instead of *because*; *in the event that* instead of *if*; *has the right but not the duty to* instead of *may*)
- unnecessary doublets and triplets (*ships, conveys, or transports* instead of choosing one and sticking with it)
- wordy nominalizations (*reached the conclusion* instead of *concluded*)
- hardcore lawyerspeak (*said* or *aforementioned* as an adjective—as in *said contract*—instead of *the*, *that*, or *this*)
- other needless language inflation (*subsequent to* instead of *after*; *effectuated service* instead of *served*)
- wordy or unnecessary prepositional phrases (*the decision of the company* instead of *the company's decision*)
- passive voice (*the motion was granted by the court* instead of *the court granted the motion*)
- excessive sentence length (you'll know)
- *shall* fever (drafters should only use *shall* when imposing a duty, and some experts disfavor the word altogether)

1. Sentence-Level Editing

1. The Contractor further agrees that the Work shall be started promptly upon receipt of such notice and shall be prosecuted regularly, diligently, and uninterruptedly at a rate of progress that will ensure full completion thereof in the shortest length of time consistent with the Contract Documents and that Contractor will cooperate and coordinate with the other City contractors or employees doing other work or using the area where Contractor is working.
2. This Contract shall be governed by, and construed in accordance with, the laws of the Commonwealth of Virginia, without application of Virginia's conflict of law provisions.

3. If any provision of this Contract, or the application of any provision hereof to a particular entity or circumstance, shall be held to be invalid or unenforceable by a court of competent jurisdiction, the remaining provisions of this Contract shall not be affected and all other terms and conditions of this Contract shall be valid and enforceable to the fullest extent permitted by law.

2. Redrafting a Contract Clause

Redraft the clause below. Beneath it, we've added some tips to help you:

SECTION 1. WORK TO BE PERFORMED AND DOCUMENTS.

For and in consideration of the money hereinafter specified to be paid by the City to the Contractor for the Work provided for in this Contract to be performed by the Contractor, the Contractor hereby covenants and agrees with the City to fully perform the services, provide any materials called for to construct, and complete the Work called for by this Contract in a good and workmanlike manner in accordance with this Contract and the documents referred to herein in order to fully and properly complete this Contract within the time stipulated, time being made of the essence for this Contract. It is also agreed by the parties hereto that the documents to this Contract consist of this Contract and the following documents listed below (Contract Documents), all of which are and constitute a part of this Contract as if attached hereto or set out in full herein. The parties agree that if there are any differences between the provisions of the above referenced documents, the provisions of the City documents and this Contract will control over any Contractor supplied documents or information.

3. Redraft Tips

1. After reading the clause once, read it again. Then again. The third time through, jot down the main ideas. Are there more than one? Does that mean that you should subdivide this into multiple sections or one main section with distinct subsections? Might your quick jots of the main ideas serve as rough headings?

2. After you've jotted down the main ideas, cut and paste the text that relates to each idea under its logical section or subsection heading.
3. After you do that, does it feel a bit less daunting to start editing the language in each piece of text? As you edit the language, be on the lookout for possible ambiguity.
4. Can you improve the typography/design? For instance, do you like the original's **ALLCAPS** heading style, or does it seem to be shouting at you? How about the **ALLCAPS** with underlining? Too visually noisy? (See Matthew Butterick's book *Typography for Lawyers* for ideas. The book is now online and free, though you might consider making a modest donation if you use it: https://typographyforlawyers.com/font-recommendations.html).
5. After you're done with your redraft, feed the original version into a generative AI program with instructions on how to improve it. Did the AI-generated redraft resemble yours?

H. A Before-and-After Case Study

Here's an example of how a typical statutory (or contract) provision can be reimagined through improved structure and plain, consistent language:

Before:

(g) A physician shall not be subject to arrest, prosecution, or penalty in any manner, or denied any right or privilege, including but not limited to civil penalty or disciplinary action by the Michigan board of medicine, the Michigan board of osteopathic medicine and surgery, or any other business or occupational or professional licensing board or bureau, solely for providing written certifications, in the course of a bona fide physician patient relationship and after the physician has completed a full assessment of the qualifying patient's medical history, or for otherwise stating that, in the physician's professional opinion, a patient is likely to receive therapeutic or palliative benefit from the medical use of marihuana to treat or alleviate the patient's serious or debilitating medical condition or symptoms associated with the serious or debilitating medical condition, provided that nothing shall prevent a professional licensing board from sanctioning a physician for failing to properly evaluate a patient's medical condition or otherwise violating the standard of care for evaluating medical conditions.

After:

(g) Protection for Physicians

(1) Scope

A physician may not be punished for giving a patient a written certification for marijuana or for concluding that the patient will benefit from marijuana. "Punished" includes being arrested, prosecuted, assessed a civil penalty, or professionally disciplined.

(2) Conditions

The protection described in subsection (1) applies only if:

(a) the patient's medical condition was serious or debilitating, and the marijuana treated that condition or its symptoms;

(b) the physician had a bona fide physician–patient relationship with the patient; and

(c) the physician fully assessed the patient's medical history before giving the written certification or diagnosing the patient's condition.

(3) Exception

Subsection (1) does not prevent a professional licensing board from sanctioning a physician who fails to properly diagnose a patient's condition or who otherwise violates the standard of care.

■ ■ ■

For more about the redrafting strategies that produced the *after* version (including confessions about why passive voice still appears, etc.), see Mark Cooney, *The Architecture of Clarity*, 9 Mich. B.J. 40 (Sept. 2016).

FOUR

Verbosity Is Verboten

A. Overview

A New York judge perhaps captured it best: "verbosity is impolite."[1] Verbosity's taxing effect on readers has spawned numerous court rules—both state and federal—aimed at preventing it. Court rules typically limit the number of pages, words, or lines allowed in a brief.[2] They may also require nonrepetitive pleadings with "clear, concise, and direct" allegations.[3]

The most notable anti-verbosity rule is probably Fed. R. Civ. P. 8, which requires plaintiffs to give "a short and plain statement of the claim."[4] This rule reflects that rambling, unwieldy complaints are "an unwelcome and wholly unnecessary strain on defendants and on the court system."[5] Defendants also

---

1. Gerald Lebovits, *The Department of Redundancy Department: Concision and Succinctness—Part I*, 78 N.Y. St. B.J. 64, 64 (July-Aug. 2006).

2. *See, e.g.*, Fed. R. App. P. 27(d)(2) (page limit for motions and replies), 32(a)(7)(A) (page limit for appeal briefs), 32(a)(7)(B) (alternative word or line limits for appeal briefs).

3. Mich. Ct. R. 2.111(A)(1).

4. Fed. R. Civ. P. 8(a)(2).

5. In re Buffets, Inc. Secs. Litig., 906 F. Supp. 1293, 1298 (D. Minn. 1995) (quoting In re GlenFed, Inc., 42 F.3d 1541, 1553–54 (9th Cir. 1994)).

must fall in line. Rule 8 compels them to state their defenses in "short and plain terms"—another unmistakable cry for brevity.[6]

Similar language appears in rules on motions and briefs. Consider this local rule for the District of Colorado: "Motions, responses, and replies shall be concise. A verbose, redundant, ungrammatical, or unintelligible motion, response, or reply may be stricken or returned for revision, and its filing may be grounds for imposing sanctions."[7]

The Federal Rules of Appellate Procedure strike the same tone. Brief-writers must give a "concise" statement of the case, a "succinct" argument summary, a "concise" standard of review, and a "short" conclusion.[8]

Litigators should view these brevity rules as allies rather than antagonists. Verbosity may be tempting, but it ultimately hurts the writer's cause. Judges buried under piles of verbose briefs may have trouble figuring out something as elementary as what issues need to be decided.[9] And writers who drown judges in "a wide sea of verbosity" make it less likely that individual claims "can be segregated for individualized analysis."[10] In other words, verbosity is verboten, unless a lawyer actually hopes to confuse readers.

B. In Pleadings

The anti-verbosity rules have teeth. Courts have struck answers containing "verbose, argumentative, and redundant statements."[11] And what about complaints that deviate from Rule 8's "short and plain statement" mandate? Here's what one court said:

---

6. Fed. R. Civ. P. 8(b)(1)(A).

7. D.C. Colo. L. Civ. R. 7.1(H).

8. Fed. R. App. P. 28(a)(6), (a)(7), (a)(8)(B), (a)(9).

9. *See, e.g.*, Lamoureux v. Anazaohealth Corp., 2009 WL 813977, at *3 (D. Conn. Mar. 26, 2009).

10. EEOC v. Corrections Corp. of Am., 2009 WL 650558, at *1 n.3 (D. Colo. Mar. 12, 2009).

11. *See, e.g.*, Temperato v. Rainbolt, 22 F.R.D. 57, 58 (E.D. Ill. 1958).

Peabody v. Griggs

2009 WL 3200686 (D.R.I. Oct. 6, 2009)

MARY M. LISI, Chief Judge.

This matter is before the Court on Plaintiffs' response to an order to show cause why their second amended complaint should not be dismissed.... [T]his Court finds that Plaintiffs have failed to show cause why the second amended complaint should not be dismissed.

I. Background and Procedural History

....

[Plaintiffs'] first amended complaint is an 18-count, 97-page, 538-paragraph document with 7 exhibits attached, totaling an additional 36 pages....

Defendants filed motions to dismiss the first amended complaint.... [T]his Court determined that the first amended complaint was in violation of the "short and plain statement" requirement of Fed.R.Civ.P. 8. This Court dismissed the amended complaint without prejudice and gave Plaintiffs until May 13, 2009, to file a second amended complaint that complied with the Federal Rules of Civil Procedure. [Footnote omitted.]

[Plaintiffs'] second amended complaint includes 13 counts laid out in 380 paragraphs over 73 pages. Additionally, 6 exhibits, totaling 22 additional pages, are attached to the complaint.... [T]his Court issued an order directing Plaintiffs to show cause in writing why the second amended complaint should not be dismissed for failure to comply with Fed.R.Civ.P. 8(a)(2)....

IV. The Second Amended Complaint

Plaintiffs contend that the complaint is lengthy because they had to reconcile the requirements of Rule 8 and Rule 9 and because the facts underlying the complaint involve a RICO claim. Plaintiffs stress that the second amended complaint is "substantially reduced in length" as compared to the first amended complaint....

Plaintiffs' assertion that the second amended complaint is substantially reduced in length misses the mark. Length alone is not the issue. This complaint is simply not a "short and plain statement of the claim." Fed.R.Civ.P. 8(a)(2). The second amended complaint contains 380 paragraphs over 73 pages and it specifically incorporates by reference 6 exhibits (22 additional single-spaced pages) containing approximately 316 additional factual averments. [Footnote omitted.] When viewed in its totality, the complaint is a rambling, fact-laden, disjointed "quagmire of minutiae." *Kuchay v. Vetter*, No. 06 C 4501, 2007 WL 2410333 at *1 (N.D. Ill. Aug. 20, 2007) (internal quotation marks and citation omitted). The complaint is replete with irrelevant, repetitive, and incomprehensible factual averments that saddle Defendants with the unfair task of meeting their obligation to "admit or deny the allegations asserted... by an opposing party." Fed.R.Civ.P. 8(b)(1)(B). The complaint also forces this Court to parse countless irrelevant and wholly unnecessary factual allegations to attempt to determine what Plaintiffs are alleging against each Defendant.

....

Plaintiffs argue that the second amended complaint is necessarily long because of the RICO claim and Rule 9's requirements. Although Rule 9 requires Plaintiffs to plead a RICO claim with particularity, Rule 9 is not a license to submit to the Court an unrestrained fact inundated opus....

This complaint is in no way, shape, or form a short and plain statement of the claim; rather, it is a conglomeration of allegations made unintelligible by its volume, morass of irrelevancies, lack of clarity and its incorporation-by-reference information overload. The complaint does not give Defendants fair notice of the claims and clearly will cause Defendants to expend significant and unnecessary effort to separate the wheat from the chaff in order to draft a reasoned response.

....

The Court therefore dismisses this complaint; such dismissal is without prejudice. Should Plaintiffs elect to file a new complaint they may do so only upon the condition that Plaintiffs first pay a counsel fee to Defendants to make them whole for the time and effort spent in responding to the first and second amended complaints. For the reasons outlined above, Plaintiffs' second amended complaint is DISMISSED for failure to comply with Fed.R. Civ.P. 8(a)(2).

SO ORDERED

Notes and Questions

1. ***Long and Laborious***: Some courts have hesitated to dismiss complaints based on verbosity alone.[12] Yet the *Peabody* court has plenty of company in opting for dismissal. For instance, in *Mann v.*

12. *See, e.g.*, Hearns v. San Bernardino Police Dep't, 530 F.3d 1124, 1131 (9th Cir. 2008).

Boatright, the Tenth Circuit affirmed dismissal because the plaintiff, a licensed attorney representing herself, filed a complaint so long and convoluted that no judge could be expected to decipher it:

> Although [the plaintiff] is a licensed attorney in the State of Illinois, she has curiously eschewed the traditional pleading style characterized by a short recitation of the facts followed by claims for relief. Instead, her first and only "Claim For Relief"... goes on for 463 paragraphs spanning 83 pages, and yet it neither identifies a concrete legal theory nor targets a particular defendant. She requests specific relief at the end of her pleading, but by this point not even the most attentive of readers could figure out who did what to whom. In short, it hardly matters whether the district court dismissed Beverly's complaint because it believed all of her claims were barred by *Rooker–Feldman* or simply because it could not separate the wheat from the chaff. It was not the district court's job to stitch together cognizable claims for relief from the wholly deficient pleading that [the plaintiff] filed. As we have frequently noted, we are loath to reverse a district court for refusing to do the litigant's job. [Footnote omitted.][13]

2. ***More Cumbersome Complaints***: Likewise, the court in *Madison v. First Magnus Financial Corp.* found that the plaintiff's first amended complaint fell "far short of satisfying the requirements of Rules 8 and 10" and was not "sufficient to survive a Rule 12(b)(6) motion to dismiss."[14] The plaintiff did "not provide a 'short and plain statement' for each claim."[15] Rather, the amended complaint was "verbose, amorphous, and conclusory, without presenting necessary facts in an understandable context."[16]

   The same was true in *Sconiers v. California Department of Social Services*, where the court found that the plaintiff's lengthy complaint violated Rule 8:

---

13. 477 F.3d 1140, 1148 (10th Cir. 2007).
14. 2009 WL 751603, at *3 (D. Ariz. Mar. 19, 2009).
15. *Id.*
16. *Id.*

> Here Plaintiff's 828-page Complaint does not adequately identify grounds for relief against Defendants to satisfy Rule 8. Plaintiff's Complaint is verbose, confusing, argumentative and conclusory. Plaintiff's Complaint fails to state the elements of her claims plainly and succinctly and to provide Defendants with fair notice.... Plaintiff's Complaint fails to comply with the short and plain statement requirement of Rule 8 as it is 828 pages in length.[17]

3. ***Decades of Dismissals***: Courts have dismissed verbose complaints across the decades. The list below offers representative examples but is by no means exhaustive. Again, none of these cases involved a pro se litigant; *attorneys* wrote these deficient complaints—and wrote too much:

1940s

Buckley v. Altheimer, 2 F.R.D. 285, 286 (N.D. Ill. 1942) (dismissing 260-page complaint containing 237 paragraphs).

1950s

Metro. Theatre Corp. v. Warner Bros. Pictures, Inc., 12 F.R.D. 516, 517–18 (S.D.N.Y. 1952) (dismissing 55-page complaint because of verbosity, redundancy, and "characterizations, lectures, dissertations, unnecessary evidence and flights of literary fancy").

1960s

Benner v. Phila. Musical Soc'y, 32 F.R.D. 197, 198 (E.D. Pa. 1963) (dismissing an amended complaint that was, among other flaws, so "prolix, argumentative and conclusionary" that the defendant couldn't possibly answer it).

17. 2008 WL 5245988, at *3 (E.D. Cal. Dec. 17, 2008).

1970s

Gordon v. Green, 602 F.2d 743, 744–46 (5th Cir. 1979) (affirming dismissal when "[t]he various complaints, amendments, amended amendments, amendments to amended amendments... total[ed] over 4,000 pages" and "require[ed] a hand truck or cart to move").

Silver v. Queen's Hosp., 53 F.R.D. 223, 225–27 (D. Haw. 1971) (dismissing a 100-plus-page complaint that was "a confusing and foggy mixture of evidentiary statements, arguments and conclusory matter").

1980s

Nevijel v. North Coast Life Ins. Co., 651 F.2d 671, 674 (9th Cir. 1981) (affirming dismissal of a 48-page complaint that was "verbose, confusing and almost entirely conclusory" and a second, 23-page complaint that was "equally as verbose, confusing and conclusory as the initial complaint").

Schmidt v. Herrmann, 614 F.2d 1221, 1224 (9th Cir. 1980) (holding that the lower court "was well within its discretion when it twice struck the appellants' pleadings," noting that "[t]his instrument alone is 30 pages in length and, it would appear that the attorney... was attempting to write a confusing statement of a non-existing cause of action rather than a 'short plain statement of the claim'").

1990s

Drysdale v. Woerth, 1998 WL 966020, at *2 (E.D. Pa. Nov. 18, 1998) (holding that a 93-paragraph complaint violated "both the letter and the spirit of Rule 8(a)(2)" because it "read[ ] more like a novel than the legal pleading it purports to be").

Kuehl v. F.D.I.C., 8 F.3d 905, 906, 908 (1st Cir. 1993) (affirming district court's dismissal of a "43-page, 358-paragraph complaint because of its failure to conform to the concise pleading requirements of Rule 8(a)").

McHenry v. Renne, 84 F.3d 1172, 1175–78 (9th Cir. 1996) (affirming dismissal of a complaint that was "argumentative, prolix, replete with redundancy, and largely irrelevant").

Vicom, Inc. v. Harbridge Merchant Services, Inc., 20 F.3d 771, 775–76 (7th Cir. 1994) (noting that it was "dismayed by Vicom's 119-page, 385-paragraph less-than-coherent amended complaint" and that the district court "should have given more serious consideration to dismissing Vicom's amended complaint with prejudice").

2000s

Brejcak v. City of Bucks, 2004 WL 377675, at *2 (E.D. Pa. Jan. 28, 2004) (striking complaint because "Plaintiff's tome span[ned] two hundred and sixteen paragraphs over forty-five pages," which "r[an] afoul of the letter and spirit of the Federal Rules").

2010s

Cafasso v. Gen. Dynamics C4 Sys., Inc., 637 F.3d 1047, 1059 (9th Cir. 2011) (affirming district court's dismissal of complaint and denial of motion to file 733-page amended complaint because "[o]ur district courts are busy enough without having to penetrate a tome approaching the magnitude of *War and Peace* to discern a plaintiff's claims and allegations").

2020s

Halstead v. Espinoza, 2021 WL 4530131, at *4–5 (N.D. Ga. Aug. 31, 2021), *aff'd*, 2023 WL 2399288 (11th Cir. Mar. 8, 2023) (denying motion to amend, noting, among other flaws, that the "[p]roposed Second Amended Complaint spans four attachments and 154-pages, which is approximately twice the length of Plaintiff's first two Complaints").

C. In Motions and Briefs

As the opinion below explains, courts typically reject briefs that exceed the word or page limit. But the consequences may be even more severe—not to mention professionally embarrassing—for lawyers who try to hide their unauthorized verbosity. When reading the case excerpt below, note that it was the renowned Judge Richard Posner, not this book's authors, who chose to identify the offending lawyer by name (starting with the early bracketed note):

Abner v. Scott Memorial Hospital

634 F.3d 962 (7th Cir. 2011)

POSNER, Circuit Judge.

[W]e issued an order to show cause why the appellants should not be sanctioned for filing an oversized brief without our permission....

The appeal is from the grant of summary judgment to the defendant in a suit under the False Claims Act. Briefs were filed at the end of last year and oral argument was scheduled for February 24 of this year before this panel. The appellants' brief states: "The undersigned [appellants' lawyer, John L. Caudill] hereby certifies that this brief complies with the type-volume limitation requirements...as this brief contains 13,877 words according to a word count by the word-processing system used to produce this brief, exclusive of sections of this brief exempted by FRAP 32(a)(7)(B)(iii)." But in note 1 on page 1 of the appellee's brief we read that the appellants' brief exceeds the 14,000-word limit—that it contains 18,000 words excluding the portions of the brief that Rule 32(a)(7)(B)(iii) exempts from the word limit. No authorization by this court had been sought or given by either party to file an oversized brief....

The appellants did not file a reply brief, so the assertion in the appellee's brief concerning the appellants' violation of the rules stood uncontradicted. That's why we issued the order to show cause "why their brief should not be stricken and/or sanctions imposed for failing to comply with Rule 32 and making a false representation to the court." After reading the appellants' response, along with the briefs, we ordered oral argument cancelled.

The response to the order to show cause, signed by lawyer Caudill, concedes that the brief exceeds the word limit (it exceeds it by more than 4,000 words), and states by way of explanation that he had "inadvertently considered only the words included in the argument section of the brief as part of the Rule 32(a)(7)(B)(iii) requirement (the word count also did not factor in citations made within parentheticals)." It is difficult to see how these errors could be "inadvertent." Rule 32(a)(7)(B)(iii) states: "Headings, footnotes, and quotations count toward the word and line limitations...." There is no ambiguity, hence no room for misinterpreting the rule as confining the required word count to the argument portion of the brief (which would, for example, allow for an endless statement of facts), or as omitting citations in parentheses.

Had appellants filed an 18,000-word brief with a truthful certificate, the brief would have been rejected; there would have been no occasion for sanctions, just as there is no occasion for sanctions when a brief is rejected for omitting a statement of the standard of review or the date on which the judgment was entered, which is essential to determining the timeliness of the appeal. We reject many briefs for these and similar reasons. The problem here, by contrast, is a misrepresentation that was initially successful in averting rejection of the brief. The misrepresentation would have gone unnoticed had the appellee not called it to our attention.

Lawyer Caudill's response to our order to show cause continues with the false claim that the appellants' violation of the Federal Rules of Appellate Procedure "came to the Court's attention via an ex parte contact made by counsel for Appellee directly to the Court of Appeals Clerk—and not (if it were actually a significant matter) in the form of a Motion filed by Appellee.... [Appellant questions] the motive of Appellee for raising it as an issue months after filing its response Brief and only eight days prior to oral argument." The appellee's brief was filed... almost two months before the scheduled date of oral argument, and it is the footnote in that brief that we mentioned earlier, not any ex parte contact with the Clerk's office, that alerted us to the appellants' alleged (and now conceded) violation of Rule 32.... We add that the appellants' brief is rambling, and would be more effective if compressed to 14,000 words. But Caudill doesn't seek an opportunity to submit a compliant brief. He insists that his 18,000+ word brief be allowed.

The response to the order to show cause, and the belated "Motion for Leave to Exceed Word Count" filed with it, advance no persuasive grounds for allowing an oversized brief to be filed, and so the brief is stricken....

We haven't found any cases in which a court dismissed an appeal for violation of Rule 32 alone. But our court and other courts of appeals as well have done so for violations of Rule 30 (or have summarily affirmed the judgment appealed from, as a sanction for such violations), which specifies requirements for the form and content of appendices to briefs....

The flagrancy of the violation in this case might well justify the dismissal of the appeal: let this be a warning. But in addition it is plain from the briefs that the appeal has no merit. To allow time for the appellants to file a compliant brief and the appellees to file a revised brief in response, and to reschedule oral argument, would merely delay the inevitable.

The motion to file an oversized brief is denied and the judgment of the district court summarily

AFFIRMED.

■ ■ ■

In a similar case, the court rejected an attorney's mathematics-defying suggestion that his "bloated" 54-page appellate brief, which exceeded the word limit by more than 3,000 words, conformed to the rules. The court still considered the appeal's merits, but that didn't help matters. As the court put it, the "seemingly interminable brief" was "wholly ineffectual":

Pierre v. MP Cloverly Partners, LP

2015 WL 6663546 (Pa. Super. Ct. Sept. 8, 2015)

Memorandum by BOWES, J.:

....

At the outset, we address Appellant's application for leave to substitute a revised certificate of compliance pursuant to Pa.R.A.P. 2135(d) for the certificate of compliance he purported to submit by way of his reply brief in contravention of the rule. As both of the certificates are defective, we deny Appellant's motion for substitution.

Pennsylvania Rule of Appellate Procedure 2135 limits the length of a principal brief to 14,000 words, and when the principal brief exceeds thirty pages, the appellant must certify with the appellate court that the brief complies with the word limitation. Specifically, Rule 2135 provides,

> A principal brief shall not exceed 14,000 words and a reply brief shall not exceed 7,000 words.... A party shall file a certificate of compliance with the word count limit if the principal brief is longer than 30 pages

> or the reply brief is longer than 15 pages when prepared on a word processor or typewriter.

Pa.R.A.P. 2135(a)(1);...

Instantly, Appellant's principal brief totaled fifty-four pages, and therefore he was required to file a certificate of compliance with this Court pursuant to Rule 2135. Appellant failed to file that document with his brief, which exceeded the limit by 3,004 words. He initially sought to remedy his misstep by attaching a purported certification to his reply brief and asking this Court to treat it as annexed to his primary brief in compliance with Rule 2135(d). However, that certification, which was procedurally and substantively defective, did not certify Appellant's compliance with the Rule 2135 or request permission to exceed the word limit. Instead, Appellant verified that he exceeded the restriction and used the reply brief as a platform to assert a litany of reasons why we should treat the brief as substantially compliant with the rule.

Thereafter, Appellant filed the instant application for leave to substitute the defective certification that he affixed to his reply brief with a new, albeit equally defective, certificate of compliance that invokes the 16,500-word limit that applies to cross appeals under Pa.R.A.P. 2136. *See* Rule 2135(a)(2). Appellant concedes the obvious fact that the instant matter does not involve cross appeals and that his brief nevertheless would exceed that increased limit. However, equating his consolidated appeal with a cross appeal, Appellant advances the innovative argument that consolidation necessitates that we allot him a 28,000-word limit, *i.e.*, double the 14,000-word limit that is typically applicable to principal briefs. Thus, by Appellant's reasoning, his bloated fifty-four paged principal brief satisfied Rule 2135 by approximately 11,000 words. For the following reasons, however, we disagree....

Stated plainly, Appellant's rationale is faulty. Generally, when this Court consolidates appeals, we direct that the matters are to be argued and briefed as one. That is, we require appellants in consolidated cases to present a single principal brief that complies with the Rules of Appellate Procedure. Nothing in the rules of procedure can be interpreted as supporting Appellant's suggestion that an appellant with consolidated cases is entitled to a relaxed word limit, much less a twofold increase in the length of the principal brief. If the Supreme Court intended for Rule 2135 to accommodate appellants in consolidated appeals similar to the exception that it carved for parties in cross appeals, Rule 2135 would express it. As the rule does not identify an exception for consolidated appeals, Appellant's argument that consolidation compels the expanded 28,000-word limit is unpersuasive.

. . . .

Moreover, we observe that Appellant's prolix brief is unwarranted because the underlying landlord-tenant action should not have spawned two lawsuits in the first place, and Appellant is solely responsible for the current procedural posture. The lawsuits involve common questions of law and fact that arose from a single landlord-tenant dispute stemming from Appellant's eviction for the nonpayment of rent. . . .

In sum, Appellant flagrantly disregarded the Rule 2135 word limit and its procedure to certify compliance. We admonish Appellant for his defiance and deny his application for leave to substitute the proposed certificate of compliance. However, since the violation of Pa.R.A.P. 2135 was not so defective so as to preclude effective appellate review, we decline to dismiss the brief or quash the consolidated appeal. . . . Although we address all of the arguments advanced in Appellant's seemingly interminable brief, we stress that his profound prolixity is wholly ineffectual.

. . . .

[After considering the appellant's various arguments on the merits, the court declares:]

In conclusion, Appellant's claims fail on all counts. . . .

Application to substitute Rule 2135(d) certificate of compliance denied. Judgment affirmed.

Judgment Entered. [Footnotes omitted.]

Notes and Questions

1. ***Taxing Readers***: A U.S. Tax Court opinion cut to the heart of why page limits exist—and underscored the folly of fudging page counts:

    > Judges impose page limits for a reason. They force parties to hone their arguments and to state those arguments succinctly. Page limits cause, or should cause, parties to dispense with arguments of little or no merit in favor of those arguments that have a better chance of carrying the day. They encourage parties to avoid redundancy. And repetition.

> Parties often are quite creative in their efforts to circumvent page limits. Among the most blatant methods is to put material into an appendix and to not count that appendix as falling within the page limits. Another is to incorporate another document by reference.
>
> Less blatant, but still obvious, are those instances in which parties shrink the margins or the font size so that they can squeeze more text within the page limits that were imposed. All of these violate Rule 23(d).
>
> Then there are methods that, while perhaps in technical conformity with our Rules, diminish the quality of a brief. Examples include moving text into footnotes or using extensive block quotations so that the author can single-space more of the text.

That excerpt is from the 2014 case *Kernan v. Commissioner*, which involved a pro se litigant. So we've strayed here from our focus on lawyer-authored documents. But this passage was too good to omit. Indeed, at least four courts (so far) have quoted it favorably.

2. ***Bloated Brief***: For a case striking a verbose brief, see *AIG Annuity Insurance Co. v. Law Offices of Theodore Coates, P.C.*, where the court struck the defendant's brief for violating a local rule requiring concise motions and responses:

> At the outset, however, I note Defendant Coates's motion violates this court's local rules requiring that "motions, responses, and replies shall be concise," and warning that "[a] verbose, redundant, ungrammatical, or unintelligible motion, response, or reply may be stricken or returned for revision, and its filing may be grounds for imposing sanctions." *See* D.C. COLO. LCivR 7.1(H) (2008).... I strike Defendant Coates's response as noncompliant with this court's local rules, but decline to return this response for refiling because, as I explain below, Plaintiff's motion for discharge is premature.... Nonetheless, I note that any future filings of this ilk, should Defendant Coates disregard my exhortations to engage separate counsel, may be grounds for sanctions pursuant to this same rule.[18]

---

18. 2008 WL 4079982, at *6, *9 (D. Colo. Sept. 2, 2008).

3. ***Criminal Verbosity***: Verbosity has also backfired on attorneys handling criminal cases. Consider *Gidney v. State*, where the court found that a criminal-defense attorney committed "an abuse of procedure" because his posttrial motion was so verbose:

   > Florida Rule of Criminal Procedure 3.850(c)(6), requires the postconviction motion to include a "brief statement of the facts (and other conditions) relied on in support of the motion." Appellant's motion and supporting memoranda of law are excessively verbose. The memoranda of law are not simply a discussion of relevant case law, but an exceedingly long and repetitious discussion of the facts supporting his claims. Because he did not paginate his memoranda of law, we can only estimate that the filing exceeds 250 pages. Considering that Gidney entered a plea in this case and that the issues he raises are not complex, his excessive motion is an abuse of procedure. There is no reason it should take several hundred pages for him to explain his claims. [Footnotes omitted.][19]

4. ***Safeguards***: How might attorneys safeguard against the type of verbosity that cost lawyers so dearly in the above cases? How might solo practitioners assess their own documents with some degree of objectivity?

5. ***Further Reading***: For more discussion and caselaw taking lawyers to task for verbosity, see Chapter 5 of Judith D. Fischer's *Pleasing the Court: Writing Ethical and Effective Briefs* (2d ed., Carolina Academic Press 2011).

D. In Contracts

A well-organized contract makes it easy for parties to find and focus on relevant provisions. So contractual verbosity might strike some as less burdensome than verbosity in court briefs, which are read from cover to cover. Yet contractual verbosity is often a symptom of poor organization and writing style, and it can make crucial provisions hard to find—and hard to understand once found.

19. 925 So. 2d 1076, 1077 (Fla. Dist. Ct. App. 2006).

For instance, a federal judge refused to enforce an arbitration clause that was buried deep inside a lengthy online contract. The contract's overall excess was a harbinger; the arbitration clause was itself a two-page wall of legalese:

Dunn v. Global Trust Management, LLC

506 F. Supp. 3d 1214 (M.D. Fla. 2020)

WILLIAM F. JUNG, United States District Judge

....

[T]he arbitration provision here is both procedurally and substantively unconscionable.

1. Procedural unconscionability.

The conditions under which Plaintiffs agreed to arbitrate their claims reflect a lack of meaningful choice. For starters, the Mobiloans application is a classic adhesion contract—a "strong indicator" of procedural unconscionability. *Gainesville Health*, 857 So. 2d at 285. The account terms are nonnegotiable. Borrowers either agree to them or they do not receive funds. These types of loans are designed for, and cater to, unsophisticated people. In an adhesion contract, the consumer lacks bargaining power, but this is especially true in the payday loan context. Prospective payday loan borrowers are often in dire straits. Outfits like Mobiloans are usually lenders of last resort that borrowers turn to only after failing to obtain a credit card or low-interest personal loan from a chartered bank. This puts the prospective borrowers in a position to accept any terms offered to them.

Compounding these pressures is how the arbitration agreement was presented. Plaintiffs were directed to the line-of-credit terms at the last step of their Mobiloans account application. To view the agreement, Plaintiffs had to open the account terms using a separate link on the Mobiloans home page. Assuming Plaintiffs opened the link, the arbitration provision is on page twelve of the account terms and itself consists of two pages of dense legalese—a lot for unsophisticated consumers to digest, particularly on their own. Presenting the arbitration provision in this way—especially given the take-or-leave-it context of the whole application process—ensures borrowers have little choice but to accept it, just as Plaintiffs did here. [Footnotes omitted.]

Notes and Questions

1. ***Concurring Opinion***: A few years before *Dunn*, a California federal judge reached the same conclusion. In *Saravia v. Dynamex, Inc.*, the court refused to enforce an arbitration-delegation clause that would have empowered an arbitrator, rather than a court, to decide whether the claim was arbitrable. The delegation clause was, in the court's words, "buried" in a lengthy form contract:

   > Moreover, this order finds that the delegation clauses in the 2011 and 2012 agreements constituted an unfair surprise exacerbating the procedural unconscionability. Nothing in the text of the agreements called Saravia's attention to the dispute resolution provisions. Those provisions were formatted identically to the rest of the provisions in the [agreements], and they lay buried in the middle of more than ten pages of mostly boilerplate language....
   >
   > This order finds that Dynamex presented the delegation provision in the 2011 agreement and the incorporation of the delegation provision in the AAA rules in the 2012 agreement to Saravia in an oppressive manner and those provisions constituted unfair surprises in the respective agreements, all amounting to procedural unconscionability.

2. ***Diagnosing Verbosity and Density***: What might lead a contract drafter to produce a document that a court refers to as "boilerplate," as in *Saravia*? Would it surprise you that a document negotiated by two (or more) attorneys could be seen as overwrought or otherwise deficient? Why or why not?

FIVE

Ambiguity (Avoiding the Interpretive Coin Flip)

A. Overview

Ambiguity exists when language forces readers to choose between two or more possible meanings—to do, in essence, an interpretive coin flip.[1] Ambiguity may add artistic depth to poems, novels, short stories, plays, paintings, or films, but it's the sworn enemy of legal writers. When drafters sow ambiguity, they relinquish control of their document's meaning. That meaning is now up to some third party, quite possibly a judge or arbitrator.

Legal drafters should take every possible step to prevent ambiguity from undermining their work. One step is to user-test every document, using clients, coworkers, consumers, or other stakeholders who come to the document with fresh eyes. Readers often spot—or get tripped up by—flaws that the drafter missed. After all, *we* always know what we mean when we write.

But the best weapon against ambiguity is knowledge. A lawyer who takes the time to understand how ambiguity arises is better positioned to spot it during the drafting process—or in a document drafted by someone else. We'll examine three types of ambiguity below, along with cases showing how courts have struggled with each.

---

1. Stephen L. Sepinuck & John Francis Hilson, Transactional Skills: How to Structure and Document a Deal 146 (2015).

B. Syntactic Ambiguity

Syntactic ambiguity, as the label suggests, arises from syntax, meaning the way in which words are arranged and relate in a sentence.[2]

Modifiers are often the culprit. For instance, if a statute applies to *licensed healthcare facilities and caregivers*, do the caregivers need to be licensed? Probably. But maybe not. The question, of course, is whether the leading (prepositive) modifier *licensed* modifies only *healthcare facilities* or modifies both *healthcare facilities* and *caregivers*. Does it reach—modify—both series items or just the single item that immediately follows it?

Likewise, trailing modifiers force readers to wonder whether the modifier modifies only the final series item or, instead, modifies every series item. For example, what if a statute defines "highway" to include "bridges, sidewalks, trailways, crosswalks, and culverts *on the highway*." Does a trailway need to be "on the highway" to fit within the definition? Or does the trailing phrase "on the highway" modify only "culverts"? Enter the last-antecedent canon. It provides that a modifier trailing a series modifies only the *final* series item. So for our hypothetical, this canon suggests that the trailing modifier only reaches the final series item, "culverts." Thus, a trailway need not be on the highway to be considered a "highway."

Yet the series-qualifier canon suggests the opposite. That canon says that if a series of nouns or verbs is straightforward and in a parallel style (i.e., each series item has the same grammatical form), then a leading or trailing modifier modifies *all* the series items, not just the item next to it. So in our hypothetical, this canon suggests that "on the highway" applies to *every* series item, including "trailways."

As it turns out, our hypothetical isn't a hypothetical. The Michigan Supreme Court had to wrestle with this very question in a real case. The court held that the trailing modifier "on the highway" reached back to every series item.[3] But this view prevailed by a whisker. Three of the seven justices preferred the opposite reading.

The United States Supreme Court's recent bout with a trailing modifier yielded similarly divergent readings:

---

2. *Id.* at 152.

3. Duffy v. Mich. Dep't of Nat. Res., 805 N.W.2d 399, 412–13 (Mich. 2011).

Lockhart v. United States

577 U.S. 347 (2016)

Justice SOTOMAYOR delivered the opinion of the Court.

Defendants convicted of possessing child pornography in violation of 18 U.S.C. §2252(a)(4) are subject to a 10-year mandatory minimum sentence and an increased maximum sentence if they have "a prior conviction . . . under the laws of any State relating to aggravated sexual abuse, sexual abuse, or abusive sexual conduct involving a minor or ward." §2252 (b)(2).

The question before us is whether the phrase "involving a minor or ward" modifies all items in the list of predicate crimes ("aggravated sexual abuse," "sexual abuse," and "abusive sexual conduct") or only the one item that immediately precedes it ("abusive sexual conduct"). Below, the Court of Appeals for the Second Circuit joined several other Courts of Appeals in holding that it modifies only "abusive sexual conduct." The Eighth Circuit has reached the contrary result. We granted certiorari to resolve that split. . . . We affirm the Second Circuit's holding that the phrase "involving a minor or ward" in §2252(b)(2) modifies only "abusive sexual conduct."

I

In April 2000, Avondale Lockhart was convicted of sexual abuse in the first degree under N.Y. Penal Law Ann. §130.65(1) (West Cum. Supp. 2015). The crime involved his then-53-year-old girlfriend. . . . Eleven years later, Lockhart was indicted in the Eastern District of New York for attempting to receive child pornography in violation of 18 U.S.C. §2252(a)(2) and for possessing child pornography in violation of §2252(a)(4)(b). Lockhart pleaded guilty to the possession offense and the Government dismissed the receipt offense.

Lockhart's presentence report calculated a guidelines range of 78 to 97 months for the possession offense. But the report also concluded that Lockhart was subject to §2252(b)(2)'s mandatory minimum because his prior New York abuse conviction related "to aggravated sexual abuse, sexual abuse, or abusive sexual conduct involving a minor or ward." . . .

Lockhart objected, arguing that the statutory phrase "involving a minor or ward" applies to all three listed crimes: "aggravated sexual abuse," "sexual abuse," *and* "abusive sexual conduct." He therefore contended that his prior conviction for sexual abuse involving an *adult* fell outside the enhancement's ambit. The District Court rejected Lockhart's argument and applied the mandatory minimum. The Second Circuit affirmed his sentence. . . .

II

The issue before us is whether the limiting phrase that appears at the end of that list—"involving a minor or ward"—applies to all three predicate crimes preceding it in the list or only the final predicate crime. We hold that "involving a minor or ward" modifies only "abusive sexual conduct," the antecedent immediately preceding it. Although §2252 (b)(2)'s list of state predicates is awkwardly phrased (to put it charitably), the provision's text and context together reveal a straightforward reading. A timeworn textual canon is confirmed by the structure and internal logic of the statutory scheme.

A

Consider the text. When this Court has interpreted statutes that include a list of terms or phrases followed by a limiting clause, we have typically applied an interpretive strategy called the "rule of the last antecedent."...The rule provides that "a limiting clause or phrase...should ordinarily be read as modifying only the noun or phrase that it immediately follows."...

The rule reflects the basic intuition that when a modifier appears at the end of a list, it is easier to apply that modifier only to the item directly before it. That is particularly true where it takes more than a little mental energy to process the individual entries in the list, making it a heavy lift to carry the modifier across them all. For example, imagine you are the general manager of the Yankees and you are rounding out your 2016 roster. You tell your scouts to find a defensive catcher, a quick-footed shortstop, or a pitcher from last year's World Champion Kansas City Royals. It would be natural for your scouts to confine their search for a pitcher to last year's championship team, but to look more broadly for catchers and shortstops.

Applied here, the last antecedent principle suggests that the phrase "involving a minor or ward" modifies only the phrase that it immediately follows: "abusive sexual conduct." As a corollary, it also suggests that the phrases "aggravated sexual abuse" and "sexual abuse" are not so constrained.

Of course, as with any canon of statutory interpretation, the rule of the last antecedent "is not an absolute and can assuredly be overcome by other indicia of meaning."...For instance, take "'the laws, the treaties, and the constitution of the United States.'"...A reader intuitively applies "of the United States" to "the laws," "the treaties" and "the constitution" because (among other things) laws, treaties, and the constitution are often cited together, because readers are used to seeing "of the United States" modify each of them, and because the listed items are simple and parallel without unexpected internal modifiers or structure. Section 2252(b)(2), by contrast, does not contain items that readers are used to seeing listed together or a concluding modifier that readers are accustomed to applying to each of them. And the varied syntax of each item in the list makes it hard for the reader to carry the final modifying clause across all three.

More importantly, here the interpretation urged by the rule of the last antecedent is not overcome by other indicia of meaning. To the contrary, §2252(b)(2)'s context fortifies the meaning that principle commands.

....

III

A

Lockhart argues, to the contrary, that the phrase "involving a minor or ward" should be interpreted to modify all three state sexual-abuse predicates. He first contends, as does our dissenting colleague, that the so-called series-qualifier principle supports his reading. This principle, Lockhart says, requires a modifier to apply to all items in a series when such an application would represent a natural construction....

This Court has long acknowledged that structural or contextual evidence may "rebut the last antecedent inference."...

But in none of those cases did the Court describe, much less apply, a countervailing grammatical mandate that could bear the weight that either Lockhart or the dissent places on the series qualifier principle. Instead, the Court simply observed that sometimes context weighs against the application of the rule of the last antecedent....

....

The dissent offers a suggestion rooted in its impressions about how people ordinarily speak and write. *Post*, at 969 – 971. The problem is that, as even the dissent acknowledges, §2252(b)(2)'s list of state predicates is hardly intuitive. No one would mistake its odd repetition and inelegant phrasing for a reflection of the accumulated wisdom of everyday speech patterns. It would be as if a friend asked you to get her tart lemons, sour lemons, or sour fruit from Mexico. If you brought back lemons from California, but your friend insisted that she was using customary speech and obviously asked for Mexican fruit only, you would be forgiven for disagreeing on both counts.

Faced with §2252(b)(2)'s inartful drafting, then, do we interpret the provision by viewing it as a clear, commonsense list best construed as if conversational

English? Or do we look around to see if there might be some provenance to its peculiarity?... [W]e are unpersuaded by our dissenting colleague's invocation of basic examples from day-to-day life. Whatever the validity of the dissent's broader point, this simply is not a case in which colloquial practice is of much use. Section 2252(b)(2)'s list is hardly the way an average person, or even an average lawyer, would set about to describe the relevant conduct if they had started from scratch.

....

D

Finally, Lockhart asks us to apply the rule of lenity. We have used the lenity principle to resolve ambiguity in favor of the defendant only "at the end of the process of construing what Congress has expressed" when the ordinary canons of statutory construction have revealed no satisfactory construction. *Callanan v. United States,* 364 U.S. 587, 596, 81 S.Ct. 321, 5 L.Ed.2d 312 (1961). That is not the case here. To be sure, Lockhart contends that if we applied a different principle of statutory construction—namely, his "series-qualifier principle"—we would arrive at an alternative construction of §2252(b)(2). But the arguable availability of multiple, divergent principles of statutory construction cannot automatically trigger the rule of lenity.... Here, the rule of the last antecedent is well supported by context and Lockhart's alternative is not. We will not apply the rule of lenity to override a sensible grammatical principle buttressed by the statute's text and structure.

....

We conclude that the text and structure of §2252(b)(2) confirm that the provision applies to prior state convictions for "sexual abuse" and "aggravated sexual abuse," whether or not the convictions involved a minor or ward. We therefore hold that Lockhart's prior conviction for sexual abuse of an adult is encompassed by §2252(b)(2). The judgment of the Court of Appeals, accordingly, is affirmed.

So ordered.

■ ■ ■

In a spirited dissent, Justice Elena Kagan stated that the Court's "ordinary understanding of how English works"—not the canons of construction—should dictate the case's outcome:

Justice **KAGAN**, with whom Justice **BREYER** joins, dissenting.

Imagine a friend told you that she hoped to meet "an actor, director, or producer involved with the new Star Wars movie." You would know immediately that she wanted to meet an actor from the Star Wars cast—not an actor in, for example, the latest Zoolander. Suppose a real estate agent promised to find a client "a house, condo, or apartment in New York." Wouldn't the potential buyer be annoyed if the agent sent him information about condos in Maryland or California? And consider a law imposing a penalty for the "violation of any statute, rule, or regulation relating to insider trading." Surely a person would have cause to protest if punished under that provision for violating a traffic statute. The reason in all three cases is the same: Everyone understands that the modifying phrase—"involved with the new Star Wars movie," "in New York," "relating to insider trading"—applies to each term in the preceding list, not just the last.

That ordinary understanding of how English works, in speech and writing alike, should decide this case. Avondale Lockhart is subject to a 10-year mandatory minimum sentence for possessing child pornography if, but only if, he has a prior state-law conviction for "aggravated sexual abuse, sexual abuse, or abusive sexual conduct involving a minor or ward." 18 U.S.C. §2252(b)(2). The Court today, relying on what is called the "rule of the last antecedent," reads the phrase "involving a minor or ward" as modifying only the final term in that three-item list. But properly read, the modifier applies to each of the terms—just as in the examples above. That normal construction finds support in uncommonly clear-cut legislative history, which states in so many words that the three predicate crimes all involve abuse of children. And if any doubt remained, the rule of lenity would command the same result: Lockhart's prior conviction for sexual abuse *of an adult* does not trigger §2252(b)(2)'s mandatory minimum penalty. I respectfully dissent....

Notes and Questions

1. ***Opposing Opinions***: Two of America's preeminent experts on legal language publicly sparred over the *Lockhart* Court's reasoning. You can find their insights—and a mock opinion by each—in these articles:

- Joseph Kimble, *How* Lockhart *Should Have Been Decided (Canons Are Not the Key)*, 101 JUDICATURE 40, 41 (2017).
- Bryan A. Garner, *How* Lockhart *Really Should Have Been Decided: Canons of Construction Are Key*, 102 JUDICATURE 56 (2018).
- Joseph Kimble, *Not So Fast: A Response to the Garner Response to My Article on* Lockhart, 102 JUDICATURE 68 (2018).

2. ***The Value of Vertical***: A vertical list can be a potent antidote to syntactic ambiguity. In fact, in both high-court cases discussed above, a vertical list surely would have made the drafters' meaning clear.

   For instance, had the drafters of the provision at issue in *Lockhart* intended for the trailing modifier to modify only the final series item, they could have signaled that by creating a vertical list and tucking the modifier into that single list item. Note that in the example below (which is a streamlined version of the statute), we've switched the list items' sequence to subtly reinforce that the modifier applies only to the single list item it's attached to:

   > (2) A person convicted of possessing child pornography in violation of 18 U.S.C. §2252(a)(4) is subject to a 10-year mandatory minimum sentence and an increased maximum sentence if they have a prior conviction under the laws of any State relating to:
   >
   > (i) abusive sexual conduct *involving a minor or ward*;
   >
   > (ii) aggravated sexual abuse; or
   >
   > (iii) sexual abuse.

   On the other hand, if the drafters had intended for the trailing modifier to modify all the series items, they could have signaled this by placing the modifier in the lead-in language that appears before the vertical list:

   > (2) A person convicted of possessing child pornography in violation of 18 U.S.C. §2252(a)(4) is subject to a 10-year mandatory minimum sentence and an increased maximum sentence if they have a prior conviction under the laws of

any State relating to any of the following offenses *involving a minor or ward*:

(i) abusive sexual conduct;

(ii) aggravated sexual abuse; or

(iii) sexual abuse.

C. Semantic Ambiguity

Semantic ambiguity arises when a word has more than one possible meaning.[4] A classic example is the word *sanctioned*:

- The board *sanctioned* his conduct.

Did the board authorize his conduct? Affirm it? (A good thing.) Or did the board punish him, as when a court sanctions an attorney for filing a frivolous lawsuit? (A bad thing—for the attorney, at least.)

Context usually resolves semantic ambiguity. (The board sanctioned the doctor's clinical trials, finding that they fell within the proper scope of his hospital privileges.) And my *sanctioned* example—a contronym with meanings on opposite poles—is unusual. Semantic ambiguity is more often about different shades of meaning.

For example, imagine an auto-insurance policy that provides coverage to an occupant who was *upon* the insured vehicle when injured.

Upon is ripe for semantic ambiguity, given its various shades or degrees of possible meaning—even when limited to notions of physical proximity:

- I sat *upon* the bench, counting butterflies. (The bench is fully and directly supporting the speaker's body.)
- At the path's end, we came *upon* a lovely brook. (The speaker could be five feet from the brook. Or two feet. Or ten feet.)

Dictionaries attest to these semantic shades. *Merriam-Webster.com* defines *upon* to mean, quite simply, "on." Likewise, *WordReference.com* defines *upon* as "up and on." *YourDictionary.com* notes that *upon* is a "somewhat elevated" version of *on* and is "generally interchangeable" with *on*.

---

4. SEPINUCK & HILSON, *supra* note 1, at 148.

So *upon* is a synonym for *on*, right? Yes. Easy enough.

But *upon*'s meaning doesn't end there. These same dictionaries also embrace the broader meaning. For instance, *Merriam-Webster.com* defines *upon* to mean that "someone or something is very close." *WordReference.com* defines *upon* as "in or into proximity with in time or space." *Dictionary.com* includes "approximate contact" as a possible meaning.

So what does it mean to be *upon* a car? Is someone one foot away from a car, preparing to change a flat tire, *upon* the car? The dictionaries give no definitive answer. In fact, they only underscore the ambiguity. You can pick your definition.

Some courts have seized on the word's broader meaning, embracing the "approximate contact" or "in proximity with" sense.[5] Other courts have gravitated to the narrower view of *upon*, refusing to bite on the word's broader meaning.[6]

Semantic ambiguity. Flip the coin.

Here's how a California appellate court decided the question:

Atlantic Mutual Insurance Co. v. Ruiz

20 Cal. Rptr. 3d 628 (Ct. App. 2004)

ELIA, J.

....

A. Stipulated Facts

Cristobol Tavares, who was driving a Toyota Camry, struck the pickup truck driven by [Robert] Ruiz and then struck a van owned by Group Manufacturing Services, Inc. of California (Group Manufacturing). Ruiz, who was uninjured at this point, exited his employer's truck and walked approximately 200 feet to where the Group Manufacturing van had stopped, to inquire about the driver's condition, to learn what had happened, and to exchange driver's license/insurance information....

Ruiz determined that the right front passenger of the Group Manufacturing van had been injured. He walked around to the passenger side door, opened the door and assisted the passenger out of the van. As he was approx-

5. See, for example, the cases cited *infra* in the Notes and Questions section.

6. *See, e.g.*, Short v. Midwest Family Mut. Ins. Co., 602 N.W.2d 914, 916 (Minn. Ct. App. 1999) (opining that broader definitions of *upon* and *on* are merely figurative).

imately one foot from the passenger door, attempting to talk with the driver, he was struck by an underinsured motorist, Alma Ogana, who was driving a minivan. Ruiz never entered Group Manufacturing's van.

....

B. Meaning of "Occupying" and "Upon" in Defining "Insured"

a. Atlantic Mutual's UM Endorsement

To be entitled to coverage under Atlantic Mutual's endorsement for uninsured motorist coverage, Ruiz had to qualify as an "insured" within the meaning of the UM coverage provisions.... [T]he term "insured" included "[a] nyone else 'occupying' a covered 'auto'" and "occupying" was further defined to "mean[ ] in, upon, getting in, on, out, or off." The question in this case is whether Ruiz was "upon" Group Manufacturing's van when he was struck by the underinsured motorist.

....

The general rules of policy construction guide our determination whether Ruiz was an insured by virtue of "occupying" Group Manufacturing's van. If the policy language is clear and explicit, it governs. *Palmer v. Truck Ins. Exchange*, 21 Cal.4th 1109, 1115 (1999). When interpreting a policy provision, we must give its terms their "ordinary and popular sense," unless "used by the parties in a technical sense or a special meaning is given to them by usage." *Id.*

A policy provision is ambiguous *only* if it is susceptible to two or more reasonable constructions despite the plain meaning of its terms within the context of the policy as a whole. *See Foster-Gardner, Inc. v. National Union Fire Ins. Co.* 18 Cal.4th 857, 868 (1998). The court may then invoke the principle that ambiguities are generally construed against the party who caused the uncertainty to exist (i.e., the insurer) in order to protect the insured's reasonable expectation of coverage. *Palmer*, 21 Cal.4th at 1115.

Where the meaning of the policy term is clear from the context of the policy as a whole, no ambiguity exists. The proper question is whether the word is ambiguous in the context of *this* policy and the circumstances of *this* case. The provision will shift between clarity and ambiguity with changes in the event at hand.

Since Ruiz was not "in" or "getting in, out or off" Group Manufacturing's van, we focus on the meaning of "upon." In everyday speech, we do not usually say a person is "upon" a vehicle. Consequently, we cannot simply look to its ordinary and popular sense and must turn to the dictionary.

"Upon" in modern usage is the equivalent of "on." *Merriam-Webster's Collegiate Dict.* 1294 (10th ed. 2001); *American Heritage College Dict.* 1482 (3d ed.1998); 2 *Compact Edition of the Oxford English Dict.* 3564 (1971). "Upon" is defined by *Oxford Dictionary* in regard to physical position (as opposed to usages involving immaterial or figurative relationships not relevant here) to mean: "Of local position outside of, but in contact with or close to, a surface." 2 *Oxford Dict., supra,* at 3564. "On" is similarly defined by *Oxford Dictionary*: "Of local position outside of, but close to or near, any surface." *Id.,* vol. 1, at 1987. This general definition includes "[i]n proximity to; close to, beside, near, by, at; on the bank of (a river or lake), on the coast of (the sea)." *Id.* at 1988.

Webster's similarly defines "on" to express physical location as follows: "1a—used as a function word to indicate position in contact with and supported by the top surface of…b—used as a function word to indicate position in or in contact with an outer surface…c—used as a function word to indicate position in close proximity with <a village ~ the sea><stay ~ your opponent>…." *Id.* at 809. *American Heritage* defines "on" in terms of physical position as follows: "1a. Used to indicate position above and supported by or in contact with: The vase is on the table. b. Used to indicate contact with or extent over (a surface) regardless of position: a picture on the wall. c. Used to indicate location at or along: a town on the border. d. Used to indicate proximity: a town on the border. e. Used to indicate attachment to or suspension from: beads on a string." *American Heritage, supra,* at 953.

Atlantic Mutual's UM policy as a whole does not clarify whether under the present circumstances "upon" is intended to convey the narrower sense of contact with a surface or a broader meaning of close physical proximity. In addition the policy does not explicitly answer whether, if the broader meaning is intended, some kind of greater connection to the insured vehicle is required beyond mere physical proximity.

....

In this case, Ruiz was positioned immediately adjacent to Group Manufacturing's van for reasons essentially related to the insured vehicle and its use on the highway. When struck by the underinsured vehicle, Ruiz was attempting to speak to the van's driver regarding the multivehicle accident that had just occurred and had just helped an injured passenger exit. In light of the principle that ambiguities in a policy are generally construed against the insurer, and the underlying public purpose of the uninsured motorist statute, we conclude that under the stipulated facts Ruiz, who was standing only about a foot from Group Manufacturing's van, was "upon" the van and qualified as an "insured" within the meaning of Atlantic Mutual's UM coverage provisions.

....

Notes and Questions

1. ***Concurring Opinions***: The *Ruiz* court's view isn't uniformly held, yet it isn't aberrant, either. For instance, an Ohio court stated that "[i]nclusion of such words as 'upon' in the definition of 'occupying' is meant to expand the terms in the definition beyond 'in,' 'on,' 'getting in,' and 'getting out' of the vehicle."[7] Thus, in Ohio a person is *upon* an insured vehicle if he or she is "within a reasonable geographic perimeter and ha[s] a relationship with" the vehicle.[8]

   An Illinois court (applying a slightly different version of the definition) held that a motorist was *upon* his car when he got out for two or three minutes, stood two to three feet in front of the car to write down his license number, and was injured when the car got rear-ended and pushed into him. After noting *upon*'s ambiguity, the court declared that the word must have been included to enlarge the concept of *occupancy*:

   > [I]t is the use of the word "upon" which creates an ambiguity. It cannot mean that the insured, to be within the meaning of the clause, had to be couched on the roof of the car or on the running board or sitting on the hood. It must connote some physical relationship between himself and the car that enlarged the area defined by the words "entering or alighting" and the word "in."[9]

2. ***A Remedy?*** What might the drafter of these insurance policies have done differently? Was the drafter's choice of the word *upon* wise? What do you think the drafter truly meant?

3. ***Consistency***: Would your answer change if you knew that the word *on* appeared in other parts of the same definition, within phrases such as *getting on*? Why would your answer change? Might your answer be an apt transition into the next section, which deals with contextual ambiguity?

---

7. Morris v. Continental Ins. Cos., 594 N.E.2d 1106, 1109 (Ohio Ct. App. 1991).
8. *Id.* at 1109–10.
9. Wolf v. Am. Cas. Co. of Reading, 118 N.E.2d 777, 780–81 (Ill. App. Ct. 1954).

D. Contextual Ambiguity

Contextual ambiguity is typically caused by inconsistent language choices within the same document or related documents.[10] It's the banana peel dropped by drafters who don't reconcile the language in associated documents or who fail to consistently use the same term to refer to the same thing. As one court observed in the insurance context, "a clear phrase within a policy can be rendered ambiguous by contradictory language elsewhere in the policy."

For instance, if a lease repeatedly refers to *outbuildings* but later throws in a reference to *ancillary structures*, shouldn't a reader presume a different meaning? After all, if the drafter had intended the same meaning, they would have used the same term, right? Drafters minimize the risk of confusion or artful advocacy by avoiding this type of inconsistency.

Consider the following case, in which documents governing a complex business deal named three different states as the proper forum for a lawsuit:

In re Sterling Chemicals, Inc.

261 S.W.3d 805 (Tex. App. 2008)

ADELE HEDGES, Chief Justice.

[R]elators, Sterling Chemicals, Inc.,... Resurgence Asset Management, L.L.C. ("RAM"), [and] Byron Haney... filed a petition for writ of mandamus in this court.... Relators ask this court to compel the respondent to enforce a forum-selection clause and dismiss the [Texas state-court] lawsuit filed by the real party in interest[, Gulf Hyrogen and Energy, L.L.C.].

We hold that the trial court did not abuse its discretion in declining to enforce an ambiguous forum-selection clause. Therefore, we deny the mandamus petition.

Background

Sterling Chemicals, Inc. manufactures and sells acetic acid and plasticizers for its customers' use in the creation of other chemicals and products. The other relators consist of some of Sterling's officers and shareholders....

Sterling entered into a Memorandum of Understanding ("MOU") with real party in interest Gulf Hydrogen and Energy, L.L.C. ("Gulf Hydrogen")

10. SEPINUCK & HILSON, *supra* note 1, at 150–51.

concerning Gulf Hydrogen's proposed acquisition of Sterling. The MOU required that Gulf Hydrogen make three non-refundable deposits of $100,000, $1,000,000, and $10,000,000 into an escrow account. In return, Sterling granted Gulf Hydrogen an exclusivity period during which Sterling would not solicit other buyers. The parties later agreed that the exclusivity period was to terminate on March 1, 2008, at which time the proposed transaction would close.

The transaction had not been complete when the exclusivity period terminated on March 1. Three days later, Gulf Hydrogen sued relators [in Galveston, Texas], alleging that (1) Haney and RAM made misrepresentations to induce it to enter into the MOU and to deposit $1,100,000 in escrow; (2) relators refused to go forward with the transaction or caused the transaction not to be completed; and (3) Sterling refused to provide and execute closing documents, as required under the MOU, although Gulf Hydrogen had already tendered performance.

Shortly thereafter, relators requested that the [Texas] trial court dismiss the lawsuit based on a forum-selection clause contained in the MOU[, which designated Delaware as the exclusive forum for resolving disputes.] ... [T]he trial court denied relators' motions to dismiss. In this original proceeding, relators assail those rulings as an abuse of the trial court's discretion.

....

Contract Interpretation

The MOU clause we have been asked to enforce provides as follows:

> All documentation in connection with the Proposed Transaction shall be governed by the internal laws of the State of Delaware, require waiver of jury trials, and consent to the State of Delaware, and the District of Delaware as being the exclusive forum for and having exclusive jurisdiction over any disputes.

The parties disagree about whether this clause applies to disputes arising from the MOU itself. In arguing that the clause unambiguously applies to the MOU as a matter of law, Sterling emphasizes the broad nature of the phrase "[a]ll documentation in connection with the Proposed Transaction." It contends that the MOU is part of "all documentation"; therefore, the argument goes, the MOU's forum-selection clause encompasses "any disputes" arising from the MOU itself. Gulf Hydrogen disagrees with this interpretation, noting that the parties expressly provided that the MOU later would be superseded by so-called Definitive Agreements:

> The parties shall negotiate in good faith to finalize the definitive agreements to give effect to the Proposed Transaction (which will supersede this MOU) on mutually agreeable terms between [Gulf Hydrogen] and [Sterling], including customary terms and as further described in this MOU (the "Definitive Agreements").

Gulf Hydrogen contends that the MOU's forum-selection clause is forward-looking and encompasses only disputes arising later after the contemplated Definitive Agreements have been created and executed. Thus, Gulf Hydrogen contends that (1) as a matter of law, the MOU's forum-selection clause is unambiguous and does not reach disputes arising from documents created before execution of the Definitive Agreements; or, in the alternative, that (2) the MOU's forum-selection clause is ambiguous, cannot be interpreted as a matter of law, and cannot serve as a basis for mandamus at this stage of the litigation.

Whether a contract is ambiguous is a question of law for the court. *J.M. Davidson, Inc. v. Webster,* 128 S.W.3d 223, 229 (Tex. 2003). We determine whether the contract is ambiguous by looking at the contract as a whole, in light of the circumstances present when the parties entered into the contract. *Universal Health Servs., Inc. v. Renaissance Women's Group, P.A.,* 121 S.W.3d 742, 746 (Tex. 2003). That the parties disagree about a contract's meaning does not render it ambiguous. *Hewlett–Packard Co. v. Benchmark Elecs., Inc.,* 142 S.W.3d 554, 561 (Tex.App.-Houston [14th Dist.] 2004, pet. denied). Rather, a contract is ambiguous when it is susceptible to more than one reasonable interpretation. *Frost Nat'l Bank v. L & F Distribs., Ltd.,* 165 S.W.3d 310, 312 (Tex. 2005). An ambiguity in a contract may be either "patent" or "latent." *Nat'l Union Fire Ins. Co. v. CBI Indus., Inc.,* 907 S.W.2d 517, 520 (Tex. 1995).

A patent ambiguity is evident on the face of the contract, while a latent ambiguity arises when a contract unambiguous on its face is applied to the subject matter with which it deals, and an ambiguity appears by reason of some collateral matter. *Id.* When a contract is found to be ambiguous, the parties' intent is a determination for the fact finder. *Coker v. Coker,* 650 S.W.2d 391, 395 (Tex. 1983). The court may conclude that a contract is ambiguous in the absence of such pleading by any party. *Sage St. Assocs. v. Northdale Constr. Co.,* 863 S.W.2d 438, 445 (Tex. 1993).

We find no patent ambiguity in the forum-selection clause.

However, when the clause is examined in light of two contemporaneous companion documents, inconsistencies between the three documents demonstrate the presence of a latent ambiguity. Specifically, this latent ambiguity becomes apparent when we examine certain provisions in the parties' confidentiality agreements and escrow agreements. When clauses in these agreements are analyzed and compared to the MOU's forum-selection clause, it becomes apparent that Sterling's "all documentation" argument overreaches.

A. Clauses in Confidentiality Agreements

Under the MOU, Gulf Hydrogen was permitted reasonable access to Sterling's personnel, property, contracts, books and records, and other such documents and data so that Gulf Hydrogen could "complete its due diligence with respect to the Proposed Transaction." The MOU also required that the parties execute one or more confidentiality agreements respecting Gulf Hydrogen's access to the documents and data. Accordingly, Sterling and Gulf Hydrogen entered into two confidentiality agreements. Both confidentiality agreements contained the following jurisdiction clause:

> Section 17. Submission to Jurisdiction. Each party hereby (a) irrevocably submits to the *non-exclusive personal jurisdiction of any Texas state or federal court sitting in Harris County, Texas,* over *any claim or dispute arising out of or relating to this Agreement* and irrevocably agrees that all such claims and disputes may be heard and determined *in such Texas state or federal court,...*

This clause contemplates that litigation of disputes relating to the confidentiality agreement will take place in Texas. Litigation in Texas is inconsistent with the MOU's forum-selection clause, which contemplates litigation only in Delaware of "any disputes" arising from "[a]ll documentation in connection with the Proposed Transaction." Logically, the confidentiality agreements could be considered part of "[a]ll documentation in connection with the Proposed Transaction," and yet those agreements contemplate litigation of disputes concerning those agreements in a forum other than the exclusive forum chosen in the MOU's forum-selection clause. This inconsistency gives rise to an ambiguity regarding the meaning of the phrases "all documentation" and "any disputes" in the MOU's forum-selection clause as the exclusive jurisdiction for "any dispute" arising out of "[a]ll documentation in connection with the Proposed Transaction."

B. Clauses in Escrow Agreements

A similar tension arises when the escrow agreements are considered. The MOU required Gulf Hydrogen to pay Sterling three non-refundable deposits of $100,000, $1,000,000, and $10,000,000. The MOU provided that the

"Non-Refundable Deposits, along with any accrued interest, will be held in an escrow ("Escrow") to be established by [Sterling] as approved by [Gulf Hydrogen] and applied to the Purchase Price at Closing." Sterling and Gulf Hydrogen entered into two escrow agreements with regard to Gulf Hydrogen's $100,000 and $1,000,000 non-refundable deposits. Both escrow agreements contained the following jurisdiction clause:

> 8. Governing Law and Counterparts. This Agreement shall be governed by and construed in accordance with the laws of New York and may be executed in separate counterparts, all of which together shall be considered as but one document. Each party shall submit to the non-exclusive jurisdiction of the courts sitting in New York.

Like the confidentiality agreements, the escrow agreements could be considered "documentation in connection with the Proposed Transaction." Thus, if the sweeping language of the MOU clause is to include the MOU itself, as Sterling claims, it likewise encompasses disputes arising from the confidentiality and escrow agreements. Yet we cannot, as a matter of law, reconcile Sterling's interpretation with the fact that the documents contain inconsistent jurisdiction provisions.

Relators contend that the confidentiality and escrow agreements should not be considered in our interpretation of the MOU clause because in each agreement, the jurisdiction clause applies only to *that* particular agreement. As a threshold matter, this contention arguably conflicts with the teaching that "instruments pertaining to the same transaction may be read together to ascertain the parties' intent." *Fort Worth Indep. Sch. Dist. v. Fort Worth*, 22 S.W.3d 831, 840 (Tex. 2000). Furthermore, this argument would not explain why the escrow and confidentiality agreements should be included in "[a]ll documentation in connection with the Proposed Transaction," including the MOU, but have their own jurisdiction clauses. Relators have argued themselves into a double blind: they cannot maintain that the MOU is part of "[a]ll documentation" such that any claims regarding the MOU fall under the exclusive jurisdiction of the court in Delaware, while at the same time assert that the other agreements—which logically could also be considered "documentation in connection with the Proposed Transaction"—should not be considered in our interpretive context. This tension cannot be eliminated by asserting that the clauses in the confidentiality and escrow agreements focus primarily on personal jurisdiction, while the MOU's clause focuses on forum. These clauses must be considered together because no purpose would be served by agreeing to the personal jurisdiction of a court located in a forum other than the exclusive forum selected by the parties.

This inconsistency among the three agreements creates a latent ambiguity in the "[a]ll documentation in connection with the Proposed Transaction" language from the MOU forum-selection clause. *See Wright v. Eckhardt*, 32 S.W.3d 891, 896 (Tex. App.–Corpus Christi 2000, no pet.). Because it is susceptible to more than one reasonable interpretation, the MOU clause is ambiguous. *See Frost Nat'l Bank*, 165 S.W.3d at 312. The forum-selection clause reasonably may be interpreted either as including the MOU itself, or as inapplicable to disputes arising before the subsequent execution of the Definitive Agreements that were to seal the transaction.

Given the ambiguity in the forum-selection clause, we cannot say that the trial court abused its discretion by denying relators' motions to dismiss.... Relators have not established their entitlement to the extraordinary relief of a writ of mandamus. Accordingly, we deny relators' petition for writ of mandamus.

Notes and Questions

1. ***AI Advantage?*** Might a commercial AI system help drafters ensure that voluminous documents are free from inconsistencies? If so, how?
2. ***AI Exercise***: Input two documents with conflicting terms into ChatGPT (or another generative-AI system) and prompt it to check for inconsistencies. Was your experiment successful? If it seems so, do you believe that your check would be finished if you were a lawyer handling this fictional transaction?

SIX

Stay Active

A. Overview

Legal writers should prefer active voice over passive voice. In fact, Justice Sotomayor is on record as saying, "Each time I see . . . the unnecessary use of passive voice, I blister."[1] She is not alone. In one survey, 23 federal appellate judges agreed that they are bothered when a brief uses passive voice.[2] And expert legal writers—people who teach and write on the subject—also prefer active voice.[3] Even clients prefer active voice.[4]

To be clear, passive voice is not ungrammatical. But passive voice is usually disfavored because it can create ambiguity or unnecessary wordiness.

What's the difference between the active voice and the passive voice? In active voice, the subject is doing the action. In contrast, passive voice promotes the target of the action to the subject position.

---

1. William Safire, *Sotomayoralities*, N.Y. TIMES (June 15, 2009), https://www.nytimes.com/2009/06/21/magazine/21FOB-safire-t.html.

2. *See* David Lewis, *If You Have Seen One Circuit, Have You Seen Them All? A Comparison of the Advocacy Preferences of Three Federal Circuit Courts of Appeal*, 83 DENV. U. L. REV. 893, 895, 906 (2006).

3. DIANA J. SIMON, THE (NOT TOO SERIOUS) GRAMMAR, PUNCTUATION & STYLE GUIDE TO LEGAL WRITING 149–50 (2022).

4. Christopher R. Trudeau, *The Public Speaks: An Empirical Study of Legal Communication*, 14 SCRIBES J. LEGAL WRITING 121, 121–22, 145 (2012).

Here's an example:

Active voice: Sylvia drove the car.

Passive voice: The car was driven by Sylvia.

Now the same example, but with internal commentary:

Active voice: Sylvia [subject] drove [verb/action] the car.

Passive voice: The car [the car gets promoted to the subject, even though it's not doing anything] was driven by [the word "by" in this style often signals passive voice] Sylvia [we finally see the actor, appearing after her action].

Another passive-voice version of this sentence removes the subject entirely, so the reader doesn't know who did the acting. With this style, the actor is implicit:

Passive voice: The car was driven.

Why is active voice preferred? In general, active voice promotes brevity and clarity, two goals in effective legal writing. Notice that in the examples above, the passive-voice versions sacrifice either brevity or clarity: in the first version, the active-voice sentence is shorter than the passive-voice sentence. The second passive-voice sentence leaves the reader to guess who drove the car, making that version less clear than its active-voice counterpart.

When would passive voice be acceptable? Passive voice can be preferable if a writer wants to de-emphasize someone's actions. For example, if you represent a criminal defendant who is accused of robbing someone, you might want to say the "property was taken" instead of saying "the defendant took the property." Similarly, politicians famously say "mistakes were made" instead of "I made a mistake." Further, if the writer does not know or care who did the acting, passive voice is appropriate. If your car was stolen, "My car was stolen" is appropriate because you do not know who stole the car, and the thief's identity is not important to the point you are making. And if you woke up one morning and found out that a mystery roommate had eaten your leftovers, you might say, "My leftovers were eaten."

Does it really matter whether you use passive voice or active voice? The short answer is *yes*. In fact, using passive voice can result in very real legal challenges and consequences. (As of this writing, a computer search for cases explicitly mentioning "passive voice" yields nearly 2,000 results.). Lawsuits have turned on the use of passive voice in many types of documents. In this chapter, we'll consider cases in which passive voice created ambiguity in statutes, contracts, and complaints. The final section will also consider the strategic rhetorical role passive voice can play in the Supreme Court's justifications for its decisions.

Practice Note

- As you read this chapter, be on the lookout for passive voice—not just in the cases, but in the prefatory comments and the notes that follow each section. When you encounter passive voice, stop and ask yourself whether it's serving an acceptable purpose. Would rewriting the passive phrases in active voice compromise accuracy? Brevity? Clarity?
- For example, one of the exercises below will challenge you to "translate" passive voice into active voice. The instructions include a passive-voice sentence. Would rewriting the sentence in active voice change its meaning or create ambiguity?

  Passive voice: Revise the sentence so that active voice is used.

  Active voice: Revise the sentence using active voice.

B. In Codified Law

Legislatures frequently use passive voice in drafting statutes, creating ambiguities that courts must then interpret—a task that could have been avoided if the legislature had used active voice.

Below are two Supreme Court decisions addressing the passive voice in statutes. In the first, the Court interpreted a federal bankruptcy provision creating an exception to the general rule allowing bankruptcy filers to discharge their debts and get a "fresh start." The statute stated that an exception exists for money obtained "by fraud," but Congress, in using passive voice, did not specify *whose* fraud it was referring to:

Bartenwerfer v. Buckley

598 U.S. 69 (2023)

Justice BARRETT delivered the opinion of the Court.

The Bankruptcy Code strikes a balance between the interests of insolvent debtors and their creditors. It generally allows debtors to discharge all pre-bankruptcy liabilities, but it makes exceptions when, in Congress's judgment, the creditor's interest in recovering a particular debt outweighs the debtor's interest in a fresh start. One such exception bars debtors from discharging any debt for money "obtained by... fraud." The provision obviously applies to a debtor who was the fraudster. But sometimes a debtor is liable for fraud that she did not personally commit—for example, deceit practiced by a partner or an agent. We must decide whether the bar extends to this situation too. It does. Written in the passive voice, [the statute] turns on how the money was obtained, not who committed fraud to obtain it.

In 2005, Kate Bartenwerfer and her then-boyfriend, David Bartenwerfer, jointly purchased a house in San Francisco. Acting as business partners, the pair decided to remodel the house and sell it at a profit. David took charge of the project. He hired an architect, structural engineer, designer, and general contractor; he monitored their work, reviewed invoices, and signed checks. Kate, on the other hand, was largely uninvolved.

Like many home renovations, the Bartenwerfers' project was bumpier than anticipated. Still, they managed to get the house on the market, and Kieran Buckley bought it. In conjunction with the sale, the Bartenwerfers attested that they had disclosed all material facts relating to the property. Yet after the house was his, Buckley discovered several defects that the Bartenwerfers had not divulged: a leaky roof, defective windows, a missing fire escape, and permit problems. Alleging that he had overpaid in reliance on the Bartenwerfers' misrepresentations, Buckley sued them in California state court. The jury found in Buckley's favor on his claims for breach of contract, negligence, and nondisclosure of material facts, leaving the Bartenwerfers jointly responsible for more than $200,000 in damages.

The Bartenwerfers were unable to pay Buckley, not to mention their other creditors. Seeking relief, they filed for Chapter 7 bankruptcy, which allows debtors to get a "fresh start" by discharging their debts. While that sounds like complete relief, there is a catch—not all debts are dischargeable. The Code makes several exceptions to the general rule, including the one at issue in this case[.]...

We granted certiorari to resolve confusion in the lower courts on the meaning of [this statute].

[W]e start where we always do: with the text of the statute...

> "A discharge under section 727...of this title does not discharge an individual debtor from any debt...
>
> > (2) for money, property, services, or an extension, renewal, or refinancing of credit, to the extent obtained by—
> >
> > (A) false pretenses, a false representation, or actual fraud, other than a statement respecting the debtor's or an insider's financial condition."

By its terms, this text precludes Kate Bartenwerfer from discharging her liability for the state-court judgment. (From now on, we will refer to Kate as "Bartenwerfer.") First, she is an "individual debtor." Second, the judgment is a "debt." And third, because the debt arises from the sale proceeds obtained by David's fraudulent misrepresentations, it is a debt "for money...obtained by...false pretenses, a false representation, or actual fraud."

Bartenwerfer disputes the third premise. She admits that, as a grammatical matter, the passive-voice statute does not specify a fraudulent actor. But in her view, the statute is most naturally read to bar the discharge of debts for money obtained by *the debtor's* fraud. To illustrate, she offers the sentence "Jane's clerkship was obtained through hard work." According to Bartenwerfer, an ordinary English speaker would understand this sentence to mean that *Jane's* hard work led to her clerkship. [The statute] supposedly operates the same way: An ordinary English speaker would understand that "money obtained by fraud" means money obtained by the *individual debtor's* fraud. Passive voice hides the relevant actor in plain sight.

We disagree: Passive voice pulls the actor off the stage. At least on its face, Bartenwerfer's sentence conveys only that *someone's* hard work led to Jane's clerkship—whether that be Jane herself, the professor who wrote a last-minute letter of recommendation, or the counselor who collated the application materials. [The statute] is similarly broad. Congress framed it to "focu[s] on an event that occurs without respect to a specific actor, and therefore without respect to any actor's intent or culpability." B. Garner, Modern English Usage 676 (4th ed. 2016) (the passive voice signifies that "the actor is unimportant" or "unknown"). The debt must result from someone's fraud, but Congress was "agnostic" about who committed it.

It is true, of course, that context can confine a passive-voice sentence to a likely set of actors. If the dean of the law school delivers Bartenwerfer's hypothetical statement to Jane's parents, the most natural implication is that Jane's hard work led to the clerkship. But in the fraud-discharge exception, context does not single out the wrongdoer as the relevant actor. Quite the opposite: The relevant legal context—the common law of fraud—has long maintained that fraud liability is *not* limited to the wrongdoer. For instance, courts have traditionally held principals liable for the frauds of their agents. They have also held individuals liable for the frauds committed by their partners within the scope of the partnership.

Understanding [the statute] to reflect the passive voice's usual "agnosticism" is thus consistent with the age-old rule that individual debtors can be liable for fraudulent schemes they did not devise.

Searching for a way to defeat the natural breadth of the passive voice, Bartenwerfer points to our observation that "'exceptions to discharge should be confined to those plainly expressed.'" This does not get her far. We have never used this principle to artificially narrow ordinary meaning, which is what Bartenwerfer asks us to do. Instead, we have invoked it to stress that exceptions should not extend beyond their stated terms....

....

All of this said, innocent people are sometimes held liable for fraud they did not personally commit, and, if they declare bankruptcy, [the statute] bars discharge of that debt. So it is for Bartenwerfer, and we are sensitive to the hardship she faces. But Congress has "evidently concluded that the creditors' interest in recovering full payment of debts" obtained by fraud "outweigh[s] the debtors' interest in a complete fresh start," and it is not our role to second-guess that judgment.

We affirm the Ninth Circuit's judgment that Kate Bartenwerfer's debt is not dischargeable in bankruptcy....

■ ■ ■

The Supreme Court faced similar challenges when construing the Sentencing Reform Act. Although the statute granted credit for time served, because of the passive-voice construction, it didn't specify who determines the credit. As you'll see below, unlike in *Bartenwerfer*, the justices didn't agree on how to interpret the Act:

United States v. Wilson

503 U.S. 329 (1992)

Justice THOMAS delivered the opinion of the Court.

A defendant convicted of a federal crime has a right under [the statute] to receive credit for certain time spent in official detention before his sentence begins. In this case, we must decide whether the District Court calculates the credit at the time of sentencing or whether the Attorney General computes it after the defendant has begun to serve his sentence....

[The defendant, Richard Wilson, was convicted of both federal and state crimes by the U.S. District Court for the Middle District of Tennessee and a state trial court. He'd been held in jail for over a year before being convicted. The District Court refused to give Wilson credit for the preconviction jail time.]

Wilson appealed the District Court's refusal to give him credit for the time that he had spent in state custody. Reversing the District Court, the United States Court of Appeals for the Sixth Circuit held that Wilson had a right to credit and that the District Court should have awarded it to him. We granted certiorari, and now reverse.

The Attorney General, through the Bureau of Prisons (BOP), has responsibility for imprisoning federal offenders. From 1966 until 1987, a provision codified at 18 U.S.C. §3568 (1982 ed.) required the Attorney General to award federal prisoners credit for certain time spent in jail prior to the commencement of their sentences. This provision, in part, stated: "*The Attorney General shall give any such person credit* toward service of his sentence for any days spent in custody in connection with the offense or acts for which sentence was imposed." (emphasis added).

In the Sentencing Reform Act of 1984, Congress rewrote §3568 and recodified it.... Unlike its predecessor, [the current version of the statute] does not mention the Attorney General. Written in the passive voice, it states:

> *A defendant shall be given credit* toward the service of a term of imprisonment for any time he has spent in official detention prior to the date the sentence commences—
>
> (1) as a result of the offense for which the sentence was imposed; or
>
> (2) as a result of any other charge for which the defendant was arrested after the commission of the offense for which the sentence was imposed;
>
> that has not been credited against another sentence.

In describing the defendant's right to receive jail-time credit in this manner, the provision has created doubt about whether district courts now may award credit when imposing a sentence. [The Court interpreted the statute's use of past ("was imposed") and present perfect ("has spent") tenses to require that a time-served credit be computed after a defendant begins their sentence, meaning district courts are unable to compute credit because of the lag between a conviction and when the defendant starts serving the sentence.]....

The United States argues that it is the Attorney General who computes the amount of the credit after the defendant begins his sentence and that the Court of Appeals erred in ordering the District Court to award credit to Wilson. Wilson counters that [the statute] authorizes the District Court to compute the amount of the credit at sentencing. We agree with the United States...that the Attorney General must continue to compute the credit under as he did under the former §3568. When Congress writes a statute in the passive voice, it often fails to indicate who must take a required action. This silence can make the meaning of a statute somewhat difficult to ascertain. Yet, even though [the statute] no longer mentions the Attorney General, we do not see how he can avoid determining the amount of a defendant's jail-time credit.

Wilson argues that our conclusion conflicts with the familiar maxim that, when Congress alters the words of a statute, it must intend to change the statute's meaning....We have no difficulty with the general presumption that Congress contemplates a change whenever it amends a statute. In this case, however, we find that presumption overcome by our conclusions that the District Court cannot perform the necessary calculation at the time of sentencing and that the Attorney General, in implementing the defendant's sentence, cannot avoid computing the credit.

We candidly acknowledge that we do not know what happened to the reference to the Attorney General during the revision. We do know that Congress entirely rewrote §3568 when it changed it to its present form.... It rearranged its clauses, rephrased its central idea in the passive voice, and more than doubled its length. In view of these changes, and because any other interpretation would require us to stretch the meaning of the words that [the statute] now includes, we think it likely that the former reference to the Attorney General was simply lost in the shuffle.

....

Reversed.

Justice **STEVENS**, with whom Justice **WHITE** joins, dissenting.

Today's rigid interpretation of a remedial statute is not supported by the text, legislative history, or underlying policies of the statute. [This] Court said that "[i]n determining the meaning of [a] statute, we look not only to the particular statutory language, but to the design of the statute as a whole and to its object and policy." The Court has failed to do this today....

....

The Court's entire analysis rests on an incorrect premise. The Court assumes that the statute mandates one of two starkly different procedures: *Either* the credit determination must *always* be made by the Attorney General after the defendant has begun to serve his sentence, *or* it must *always* be made by the sentencing judge at the time of sentencing. Neither of these procedures is compelled by the statutory text. An ordinary reading of the statute's plain language ("[a] defendant *shall be given* credit toward the service of a term of imprisonment...") suggests that the judge has ample authority to delegate the task of calculating the credit to a probation officer or to the prosecutor, subject, of course, to judicial review, or to make it himself in the first instance. Surely there is nothing in the statutory text that purports to deprive the judge of discretion to follow whichever procedure seems best suited to the particular facts of a given case. The text, which uses the passive voice, does not specify who will make the decision about jail credit. Certainly we should give effect to Congress' choice of words, and understand that the text, as written, does not identify a particular decisionmaker, and therefore, the appropriate decisionmaker may be *either* the judge or the Attorney General depending on the circumstances.

....

For the foregoing reasons, I would affirm the judgment of the Court of Appeals.

Notes and Questions

1. ***Passive Jurisprudence***: Does the Court treat passive voice consistently in *Bartenwerfer* and *Wilson*? How would you explain the Court's approach to resolving the ambiguity in each case? Did the Court use common law, canons of construction, precedent, or other interpretive tools? Can you come up with a single theory that explains the outcome in both cases?

2. ***Legislative Solution?*** In *Bartenwerfer*, Justices Sotomayor and Jackson concurred in the judgment. The concurrence noted that fraud under the common law encompassed "agency and partnership principles," and that the Court's decision did not involve "fraud by a person bearing no agency or partnership relationship to the debtor."[5] If you were in Congress and wanted to rewrite the bankruptcy statute discussed in *Bartenwerfer*, how would you rewrite it so that it would unambiguously *include* actors like Kate Bartenwerfer but *exclude* actors who have no agency or partnership relationship to the person committing the fraud?
3. ***Be a Tenth Justice***: In *Wilson*, do you agree with the majority opinion or the dissenting opinion? Why?
4. ***Passive Predicament***: The Americans with Disabilities Act of 1990 generally prohibits employment discrimination against disabled employees. Under a catchall provision, Congress provided that it is "unlawful to coerce, intimidate, threaten, or interfere with any individual in the exercise or enjoyment of" a protected right. One plaintiff was fired after suffering an accident. Instead of suing her employer, she sued a party *who was not her employer*. She argued that the statute was not limited to suits against employers. The Sixth Circuit phrased the issue as follows: "Does this passive voice construction mean that a disabled individual may sue anyone—from a close friend to a complete stranger—who happens to interfere with an ADA protected right? Say, for example, someone parks in the individual's designated handicapped spot at work. Is the culprit liable under the ADA?"[6] How do you think the court ruled? How would you reword the statute to avoid the passive voice?
5. ***A Known Secret?*** A defendant was convicted for unlawfully recording a conversation between himself and a police officer. Specifically, the defendant was pulled over by a police officer, and the officer informed the defendant that the conversation was being recorded. Unbeknownst to the officer, the defendant also recorded the encounter with his cell phone. When the officer realized that the defendant had recorded the conversation, the defendant was arrested

---

5. 598 U.S. at 83–84 (Sotomayor, J., concurring).
6. Post v. Trinity Health Mich., 44 F.4th 572, 576 (6th Cir. 2022).

for recording the conversation. The relevant statute provided that a person may not "[o]btain ... the whole or any part of a conversation by means of any device ... if not all participants are specifically informed that their conversation *is being obtained*." On appeal, the defendant argued that notice is notice—the statute did not require specific people to give the notice, and the officer had effectively notified both the defendant and (of course) himself that the exchange was being recorded. The court transitioned into its analysis with this observation: "Generally, where the legislature employs the passive voice with regard to an action that a statute either authorizes or requires ... that usage indicates an intention to avoid specifying a particular actor to whom the statute's command is directed."[7] Do you think the defendant's argument prevailed? Should it have?

6. ***Shortfall Windfall?*** The widow of a deceased coal miner sued her late husband's employer seeking additional compensation under a statute that provides as follows: "If any compensation, payable under the terms of an award, is not paid within ten days after it becomes due, there shall be [additional compensation paid]." The Drummond Company, which had employed the plaintiff's husband, admitted that it failed to pay the plaintiff within ten days. But the Black Lung Disability Trust Fund, which "exists to pay benefits if no responsible coal mine operator can be identified or if the operator fails to pay benefits after they become due," had covered the shortfall. Drummond argued that because the Trust Fund had paid, the plaintiff had no right to additional compensation under the statute. The court noted that the statute's "use of the passive-voice phrase 'is not paid' complicat[ed] what would otherwise be a straightforward exercise in statutory interpretation."[8] The issue was thus whether the statute required additional compensation whenever an award is not paid by the responsible operator (here Drummond), even if some other entity does pay the benefits. How do you think the court ruled? How should it have ruled? How could the statute be rewritten to make clear who must pay the compensation?

---

7. State v. Neff, 265 P.3d 62, 65 (Or. Ct. App. 2011).

8. Burton v. Drummond Co., 350 F. Supp. 3d 1198, 1206 (N.D. Ala. 2018).

7. ***Source of Notice***: Under Michigan law, someone injured through a government agency's conduct must give written notice to the agency before they can sue. The relevant statute provides that "written notice of any claim based upon injury to persons or property shall be served upon the authority no later than 60 days from the occurrence...." Assume that an agency learns of a plaintiff's injury through police reports and its own internal documents, but the plaintiff doesn't serve written notice. Should the court dismiss the plaintiff's suit even though the agency actually knew of her claim through its own resources?[9]

C. In Contracts

Passive voice has also sparked litigation based on dueling interpretations of ambiguous contract provisions. Usually, these cases involve contracts that provide *what* must be done but fail to specify *who* must do it. In interpreting contracts, courts commonly apply *contra proferentem*, a maxim stipulating that ambiguities are generally construed against the contract's drafter. Drafting unambiguous contracts is therefore of critical importance. As discussed below, however, there is room for passive voice in a contract when its use would be advantageous to one party or another because it imposes broader duties.

In the first case below, the court considered a contract that allowed for removal of certain insurance policies in a trust but failed to specify which party had authority to remove the policies. The contract concerned niche financial instruments, so the case is challenging. But focus on the core passive-voice issue: Which party had removal power?

SEC v. Mutual Benefits Corp.

2020 WL 5259162 (S.D. Fla. Sept. 3, 2020)

STRAUSS, Magistrate Judge.

[Acheron Capital bought 100% of the ownership interest in several insurance policies owned by a trust. In March 2015, the trustee and Acheron entered into an agreement governing those policies. Later, the trustee asked the court to remove

9. *See* Fields v. Smart, 874 N.W.2d 715 (Mich. Ct. App. 2015).

the Acheron-owned policies from the trust, transferring ownership to Acheron, and also to authorize the trustee to remove such policies in the future.]....

The parties' dispute as to... removal has centered on passive language that is found in Section 6 of the March 2015 Agreement, which states:

> 6. Removal of Policies From Trust. To the extent not already permitted, any policy as to which Acheron has acquired 100% of the interests *may be removed* from the Trust.

Because of the passive language, the provision does not explicitly state who can do the removing.

Here, the language at issue, while not defective, obscure, or insensible, fails to explicitly denote the rights or duties of the parties when they are not in agreement regarding removal of the policies. Finding that, alone or in combination, other provisions of the March 2015 Agreement and the parties' course of performance do not clarify the parties' intent sufficiently to overcome the Removal Provision's use of passive voice, I conclude that a latent ambiguity exists, and that extrinsic evidence should be considered to construe it. Indeed, I find that there are four potential ways to interpret "may be removed" in the Removal Provision as it applies to the 100% Acheron-owned policies:

1. It confirms that the parties, when in agreement, can remove the 100% Acheron-owned policies; otherwise, the policies remain in the Trust.

2. It provides Acheron the sole unilateral right to remove, or not remove, the 100% Acheron-owned policies;

3. It provides the Trustee the sole unilateral right to remove, or not remove, the 100% Acheron-owned policies, or it confirms the Trustee's pre-existing right to do so;

4. It provides both parties a right to unilaterally remove the 100% Acheron-owned policies, or it confirms Acheron's right while also preserving the Trustee's pre-existing right to do so;

Finally... Acheron was the primary drafter of the provision and should bear the consequences of the Removal Provision's ambiguous language.... Here, Acheron's attorney acknowledged drafting and proposing the Removal Provision with the passive language at issue, which passive language was incorporated into the final agreement. Therefore, I conclude that Acheron is the drafter of the ambiguous language. Further... any ambiguity remaining after other rules of construction are applied is construed against Acheron under Florida law....

Accordingly... the Trustee's Motion to Remove is GRANTED. The parties shall cooperate to accomplish removal of Acheron's 100% owned policies that are held by the Trust, in conformance with the March 2015 Agreement's Removal Provision, as soon as practicable.

■ ■ ■

Similarly, passive voice in a noncompete agreement resulted in a disagreement about when the noncompete would terminate: when the employer fired the employee or when the employee left voluntarily.

East Texas Copy Systems, Inc. v. Player

528 S.W.3d 562 (Tex. Ct. App. 2016)

Opinion by Justice MOSELEY

[The defendant, Jason Player, sold his business to the plaintiff, Copy Systems, and, in doing so, entered into an asset-purchase agreement. The agreement prohibited Player from engaging in a competing business. The parties also signed a noncompete agreement. As part of the asset-purchase agreement, Copy Systems hired Player. Two years after signing the agreement, Player resigned and immediately resumed business in competition with Copy Systems. Player filed suit, asking the court to declare that he had a right to compete, and Copy Systems filed a counterclaim to enforce its interpretation of the noncompete agreement. The trial court held that Player could compete. Copy Systems appealed. The court of appeals affirmed.

The asset purchase agreement provided, in part, as follows:]

> Upon finalizing this transaction, the Seller will not directly or indirectly engage in any business competitive with the type of business Jason Player is engaged in prior to this Agreement other than his employment with Buyer for a period of two years.... *If Jason Player's employment with Buyer is terminated prior to two year* [sic] *from the date of this Agreement for any reason other than a for cause termination, this Non-Compete clause will no longer be binding.*

(Emphasis added)

....

The parties do not dispute that Player's employment was terminated prior to July 1, 2015, without cause. Rather, Copy Systems argues that the Disputed Clause should be interpreted to only be effective if Copy Systems terminated Player's employment.

We agree with the trial court that under the plain and ordinary meaning of the terms used in the parties' agreement, the Disputed Clause was effective if either party terminated Player's employment. Under the employment contract, both Copy Systems and Player were given the right to terminate Players' employment by giving sixty days written notice to the other party. Thus, under the parties' agreement, either Copy Systems or Player could terminate his employment. Significantly, the Disputed Clause simply says that the triggering event is that "[i]f [Player's] employment with Buyer is terminated (without cause)," without identifying which party terminates the employment relationship. Thus, the emphasis of the Disputed Clause is on the termination of Player's employment, not which party initiates the termination. Under the parties' agreement, either party could terminate the employment relationship. Therefore, we presume that the parties, by not limiting which party initiates the termination, intended that either party could initiate the termination. Since Player's employment was terminated prior to July 1, 2015, without cause, the non-compete clauses... were no longer binding.

Notes and Questions

1. ***Court Consistency?*** In *SEC*, the court construed the contract against the drafter and held that the trustee had the right to remove the policies. But in *East Texas Copy Systems, Inc.*, the court held that the noncompete expired regardless of which party terminated the contract. Are these decisions consistent? Why or why not?
2. ***Capturing Intent***: Do you think the buyer in *East Texas Copy Systems, Inc.*, intended for Player to be able to compete even if he resigned instead of being fired? How could the company's lawyer have drafted this provision to ensure that Player could only compete if East Texas Copy Systems fired him?

3. ***Positively Passive?*** Sometimes, the use of passive voice is appropriate in a contract.[10] Why? In what circumstances might passive voice be beneficial? Evaluate these hypotheticals as to whether passive voice is preferable or not.

   a. You're buying equipment, and the agreement contains this clause about prior ownership of the equipment: "The equipment was purchased new from an authorized dealer." Does this sentence use the passive voice? As the purchaser, do you want this sentence revised to say that "Seller purchased the equipment new from an authorized dealer." Why or why not?

   b. You're buying a car. The car has had more than one previous owner. The sale agreement provides that "[t]he car has only been driven 20,000 miles since seller bought it." Does this sentence use active or passive voice? If you represent the buyer, do you prefer active or passive voice for the car's mileage? Does the provision give the buyer all the information she needs? How would you revise this sentence?

   c. You're drafting an insurance policy providing coverage for "temporary workers" furnished to an employer to meet seasonal or short-term workload conditions. The insurer only wants to provide coverage when a third party, such as a staffing agency, furnishes the employee. The insurer does not want to cover those situations in which an employer hires someone like a friend to do the work. How would you draft this provision? Assume that you draft a provision as follows: A "temporary worker" is "a person who is furnished to [an employer] to substitute for a permanent 'employee' on leave or to meet seasonal or short-term workload conditions." Does this clause limit temporary workers to those that staffing agencies supply? How might a court interpret this clause if the temporary worker were a friend?[11]

---

10. Stephen L. Sepinuck, *So Let It Be Written: When to Use the Passive Voice in Contract Documents*, 7 TRANSACTIONAL LAW. 2 (2017).

11. *See* Kemp v. Allen, 2017 WL 2463399 (Mich. Ct. App. June 6, 2017).

D. In Pleadings

Pleading in the passive voice has also led to severe consequences. In the first case below, the court dismissed the plaintiffs' civil-rights complaint because by using the passive voice, the plaintiffs did not specify who did what—only that actions were taken. More specifically, the plaintiffs alleged false arrest and malicious prosecution after being arrested and charged with multiple misdemeanors related to animal cruelty. The statute providing for private civil-rights claims against government officials requires claimants to identify specific actions made by particular officials. A viable claim cannot rest on generic or nonpersonalized allegations of wrongdoing:

Fullen v. City of Salina

2021 WL 4476780 (D. Kan. Sept. 30, 2021)

JULIE A. ROBINSON, Chief United States District Judge

....

[The plaintiffs allege that they] "were arrested," then were "held in the Saline County jail for over 48 hours prior to being charged with multiple misdemeanors in connection with false allegations of animal cruelty," and then "were maliciously prosecuted at the insistence of City personnel." Plaintiffs claim that, "[a]s a direct and proximate result of the wrongful actions of the defendants Salina, the Sheriff, their employees, agents and the other individual defendants, plaintiffs Matthew Fullen and Beverly Fullen were wrongfully and maliciously prosecuted."

These allegations are insufficient to make out viable [section 1983] claims for false arrest and malicious prosecution against any Defendant, and thus do not survive assertions of qualified immunity. The Petition is riddled with allegations in the passive voice and makes collective and conclusory allegations unsupported by specific factual allegations. The Tenth Circuit has stressed that "it is incumbent upon a plaintiff to 'identify specific actions taken by particular defendants' in order to make out a viable [section 1983] ... claim." Given that requirement, a "plaintiff's facile, passive-voice showing that his rights 'were violated' will not suffice...."

Plaintiffs' failure to make a "more particularized, defendant-specific" showing both "dooms" the false arrest and malicious prosecution claims and entitles the Officers and Cowie to qualified immunity. The Court therefore dismisses Beverly Fullen's and Matthew Fullen's... claims for false arrest and malicious prosecution.

■ ■ ■

In the next case, the plaintiff's complaint was also dismissed because of passive voice. This time, the issue was personal jurisdiction. The plaintiff, a company that supplies medical equipment to healthcare providers and government bodies in the U.S., sued two distributors for selling it counterfeit surgical masks. The complaint alleged that items "were shipped" but didn't say which entity shipped them. The defendants moved to dismiss the complaint, arguing that the court lacked personal jurisdiction. The court granted the motion and rejected the plaintiff's argument:

Alkali Scientific, LLC v. Wang

2022 WL 4484071 (D. Md. Sept. 27, 2022)

GEORGE L. RUSSELL, III, United States District Judge

....

[Plaintiff] contends that this Court has personal jurisdiction over [Defendants] because "the masks sold to it in Maryland were imported by [Defendants] and at least the first lot was provided to [Plaintiff] in Baltimore." That does not appear to be so. First, [Plaintiff] does not plead that [Defendants] were responsible for shipping any masks to Baltimore in its Amended Complaint. Indeed, [Plaintiff] alleges only that, "[u]pon information and belief, some of the masks <u>were shipped</u> from that warehouse to... Baltimore, Maryland." [Plaintiff's] sly use of the passive voice in its drafting of the Amended Complaint leaves out the existence of any specific actor responsible for the Baltimore shipment, let alone [Defendants]. This is insufficient to demonstrate personal jurisdiction. See Cloninger v. Harvey, No. CV 3:20-0170, 2020 WL 2559949, at *4 (S.D.W. Va. May 20, 2020) ("[T]he complaint uses the passive voice to evade specifying the conduct of each defendant. This runs afoul of Federal Rule of Civil Procedure 8(a)(2)'s requirement of a 'short and plain statement of the claim....'" (citation omitted)). [Underlining in original.]

....

Notes and Questions

1. ***Why Passive?*** Why would a plaintiff use passive voice instead of active voice when drafting a complaint? Are there circumstances in which such a complaint would, unlike the complaints in the above cases, survive a motion to dismiss?

2. ***Unattributed Assurances***: Assume that when suing for wrongful termination on due-process grounds, a former at-will employee (meaning one who could be fired at any time) alleged that "[s]he was assured that she would continue on the job as long as she performed satisfactorily." Assume also that the defendants moved to dismiss, arguing that the former employee failed to allege a cognizable property interest in her continued employment. Do you think the court would have granted the motion to dismiss? Why or why not?[12]

3. ***Other Filings***: What about other kinds of court filings? Does passive voice matter in those? Assume that a party invokes the attorney-client privilege to protect a PowerPoint document. The supporting declaration states that the document "was revised" and "was presented" during a management meeting. But the declaration doesn't state who prepared the document or who presented it. Is the court likely to conclude that the document is protected from disclosure because of the attorney-client privilege? Why or why not?[13]

4. ***Passive Voice and the Judicial Branch***: As discussed above, passive voice can be used for strategic reasons, and even the Supreme Court has used passive voice as a rhetorical strategy.[14] Some commentators believe that the Court uses passive voice when rationalizing its forays into politically charged cases.[15] For instance, in *Citizens United v. Federal Election Commission*, the majority opened its opinion as follows: "In this case we are asked to recon-

---

12. *See* Ponder v. Cnty. of Winnebago, 2021 WL 3269842 (N.D. Ill. Sept. 30, 2021).

13. *See* Elsasser v. Devon Energy Prod. Co., 2022 WL 17488164 (D. Wyo. Dec. 7, 2022).

14. Daniel Skinner & Steven Pludwin, *The U.S. Supreme Court and the Politics of Passive Writing*, 45 POLITY 499, 513 (Oct. 2013).

15. *Id.*

> sider *Austin* and, in effect, *McConnell*."[16] The dissent balked at the notion that the Court was impelled by some unnamed, unknown actor to decide the matter. Justice Stevens and his fellow dissenters quipped that their "colleagues' suggestion that 'we are asked to reconsider *Austin* and, in effect, *McConnell*,' ... would be more accurate if rephrased to state that 'we have asked ourselves' to reconsider those cases."[17]

Passive voice plays a role in judicial decision-making at every level. Think about opinions you've read: How do judges interpret and apply statutes, common-law standards, or precedent? How do they write about it? Do they suggest that they are merely acting as objective or neutral referees, bound to apply existing law as it is? Keep an eye out when you read opinions—you may be surprised by how often judges use passive voice to de-emphasize their agency in construing or applying the law.

E. Exercises

Do any of the sentences below use passive voice? If so, convert the sentence to active voice.

1. It was held that the claim amounts were uncertain and thus did not satisfy the specific-amount requirement.
2. Because the wording of the draft notice is vague, it would result in the notice's being found insufficient.
3. It was reasoned that the notice only contained an invitation to bargain.
4. The notice must make it known that the claimant is seeking an amount that will settle the case before trial.
5. The book was written by the plaintiff while working for the defendant.

The following sentences use passive voice. Decide whether they should be revised to use the active voice, and if so, rewrite them accordingly.

---

16. 558 U.S. 310, 319 (2010).

17. *Id.* at 396 (Stevens, J., concurring in part and dissenting in part).

1. Substantial monies were borrowed from my political campaign.
2. A member of my staff was touched in an inappropriate fashion.
3. At the time the store was being robbed, the defendant was sitting at home watching television.
4. The plaintiff was struck by falling debris and thus pleads a claim for negligence.

SEVEN

Avoid Run-on Sentences

A. Overview

For this chapter, we'll use the phrase "run-on sentence" in the way that most people use it—as a shorthand reference to long, convoluted sentences. Technically, a run-on sentence is one in which independent clauses are fused together without any punctuation or coordinating conjunction.[1] Some of the offending sentences in the cases discussed below, though vexing, don't fit that definition.

Run-on sentences can come back to bite litigators and transactional attorneys alike. For litigators, run-on sentences can undermine motions and briefs, clouding arguments and eroding credibility.[2] The same is true for discovery requests. Consider, for example, the party whose discovery request failed because it described the sought-after documents "in a single, run-on sentence covering more than a full page and including a non-exclusive ('without limitation') listing of 24 separate types of information."[3] This rambling definition

---

1. *See* Bryan A. Garner, Garner's Dictionary of Legal Usage 792 (3d ed., Oxford U. Press 2011).

2. *See, e.g.*, Cal. DHI, Inc. v. Erasmus, 2008 WL 821778, at *5 (D. Colo. Mar. 26, 2008) ("This argument is difficult to parse: each paragraph consists of a single run-on sentence, and the verb tenses and apparent subject of each sentence shift abruptly and repeatedly.").

3. In re Pabst Licensing GmbH Patent Litig., 2001 WL 797315, at *19 (E.D. La. July 21, 2001).

was "so complex, broad and burdensome on its face," the court observed, "as to defy either a rational response by parties receiving these requests or an evaluation by this court."[4] Another court sanctioned a party $2,500 for blocking discovery with vexatious nonresponses, the most notable being an interrogatory answer that contained multiple objections followed by "a few turgid run-on sentences that would cause a high school English teacher to blush."[5]

For legal drafters, run-on sentences jeopardize clarity and, in some cases, enforceability. For instance, a court may be reluctant to enforce a potentially harsh contractual provision, such as an indemnity clause in a consumer document, if that provision is "buried at the end of a run-on sentence."[6] Even attempts at plain-language releases can be undone by sentence length. The Wisconsin Court of Appeals refused to enforce release language couched in "a 176-word run-on sentence."[7] Even though the sentence was "not packed with legalese," it still lacked clarity and thus did not unambiguously encompass the accident at issue.[8]

Below, you'll see more examples of documents—and cases—crashing under the weight of oversized sentences.

B. In Pleadings

As noted in previous chapters, the Federal Rules of Civil Procedure demand brevity and clarity. Under Rule 8, for example, a complaint "must" contain a "short and plain statement of the claim." That rule's mandatory *must* is conspicuously not a discretionary *may*. No wonder federal courts hang the "requirement" tag on Rule 8's call for plain language.[9]

---

4. *Id.*

5. Trafton v. Rocketplane Kistler, Inc., 2009 WL 2251288, at *1 (E.D. Wis. July 22, 2009).

6. Madsen v. Wyo. River Trips, Inc., 31 F. Supp. 2d 1321, 1324 (D. Wyo. 1999) ("But this indemnification provision was buried at the end of a run-on sentence (in very small print) in which the entire focus of the sentence was that Mr. Madsen was only signing on behalf of he [sic] and his minor children.").

7. Cass v. Am. Home Assur. Co., 699 N.W.2d 254, 2005 WL 1119783, at *2 (Wis. Ct. App. 2005).

8. *Id.*

9. Ong v. Park Manor (Middletown Park) Rehab. & Healthcare Ctr., 51 F. Supp. 3d 319, 343–46 (S.D.N.Y. 2014).

State court rules from across the country sing the same tune. Alabama Rule of Civil Procedure 8(a), like its federal counterpart, requires a "short and plain statement of the claim." Michigan's court rules state that allegations "must be clear, concise, and direct."[10] New Jersey requires "simple, concise and direct" allegations.[11]

Yet court pleadings often call to mind very different adjectives. Many lawyers, it seems, ignore the rules' letter and spirit, falling back to so-called traditional style or a more-is-better approach—with much of the excess appearing in seemingly unending sentences. This carries some risk. Even judges who are tolerant of legal long-windedness have a breaking point, and the pleading rules have teeth. An attorney might lose a case—more accurately, might lose a *client's* case—for flouting the rules' call for a direct, clear style.

Halstead v. Espinoza

2021 WL 4530131 (N.D. Ga. Aug. 31, 2021)

STEVE C. JONES, United States District Judge

This matter appears before the Court on Defendants' Motions to Dismiss....

....

II. LEGAL STANDARD

Under the Federal Rules of Civil Procedure, a complaint must contain "a short and plain statement of the claim showing that the pleader is entitled to relief." Fed. R. Civ. P. 8(a)(2). The purpose of this requirement is "to give the defendant fair notice of what the claim is and the grounds upon which it rests." *Bell Atl. Corp. v. Twombly*, 550 U.S. 544, 555 (2007) (quotation marks omitted and alteration adopted)....

Federal Rule of Civil Procedure 41(b) permits a defendant to move to dismiss an action where "the plaintiff fails to prosecute or comply with these rules or a court order...." Fed. R. Civ. P. 41(b)....

10. Mich. Ct. R. 2.111(A)(1).

11. N.J. Ct. R. 4:5-7.

III. DISCUSSION

For the following reasons, the Court concludes that Plaintiff's First Amended Complaint is due to be dismissed.... It also concludes repleading would be futile.

A. Plaintiff's First Amended Complaint Fails to Comply with Both Federal Rule of Civil Procedure 8 and this Court's Previous Order

Plaintiff was already given one opportunity to replead his claims, with specific instructions from the Court. He failed to do so....

First, Defendant argues, and the Court agrees, that Plaintiff's First Amended Complaint is drafted in a way that renders it "nearly impenetrable." Doc. No. [26-1], 6. The myriad grammatical errors, confusing sentence structure, and run-on sentences make it extremely difficult to decipher. To take one example, the first sentence of the "Introduction" states:

> This case seeks to vindicate the Eleventh Amendment §1983 employment practices that violated Plainitff [sic] HALSTEAD'S Constitutional Rights & Fourteenth Amendment rights of the Plaintiff to Due Process of Law with its Protections, and a Title 18 claim under §242, and Tort and common law claims for Intentional infliction of emotional distress, Defamation, assault and battery, et al. [sic] and all other Constitutional Amendments not heretofore mentioned, as a Decorated Law Enforcement officer who was subjected to horrendous hostile work environment, deprivation of due process and his Constitutional Rights and Privileges and Harassment/sexual harassment by his supervising officer, ESPINOZA, and others working in concert with him to deny Halstead his Constitutional Rights and privileges.

Doc. No. [25], 2. This 116-word sentence is so difficult to follow, it fails to provide fair notice of the nature of the claims....The First Amended Complaint is riddled with such convoluted sentences.

Second, Plaintiff failed to provide separate, simple, concise, and direct statement of each of Plaintiffs' claims for relief, as ordered. *See* Doc. No. [23], 6. Indeed, Plaintiff committed—for the second time—the "mortal sin" of shotgun pleading: "multiple counts where each count adopts the allegations of all preceding counts, causing each successive count to carry all that came before and the last count to be a combination of the entire complaint." *Weiland*, 792 F.3d at 1321....

Third, Plaintiff's paragraphs are still not limited to a single set of circumstances; nor are the circumstances that apply to a particular claim for relief set forth under each claim for relief. *See* Doc. No. [23], 6 (ordering Plaintiff to provide "separate, simple, concise, and direct statement of each of Plaintiffs' claims for relief" and "[n]umbered paragraphs limited to a single set of circumstances, with only the circumstances that apply to a particular claim for relief set forth under each claim for relief"). As before, the First Amended Complaint is "rife with conclusory allegations and facts seemingly irrelevant to the information at the beginning of the paragraph." *Id.* at 5. Plaintiff continues to cross-reference different claims and legal theories in his various counts and causes of action, with vague references to extraneous "facts." The alleged facts do not appear to be chronological, but rather skip around in time with few or no dates certain provided. It remains entirely unclear what alleged facts support which claims for relief.

Fourth, while some claims are now clearly brought against particular Defendants, others remain unclear....

Finally, the Court finds that the scope of Plaintiff's First Amended Complaint is improper. As Defendants note, an order granting a defendant's motion for more definite statement is not an opportunity for the plaintiff to add new claims or parties....

B. Allowing Plaintiff to Replead Again Would Be Futile

Nor is repleading likely to cure the First Amended Complaint's many deficiencies. Indeed, Plaintiff has already shown this Court what a second attempt at repleading would look like in the Proposed Second Amended Complaint attached to his Motion to Amend.... It does not remedy any of the above-mentioned deficiencies—if anything, it exacerbates them....

Plaintiffs Second Amended Complaint is a step away from—not toward—compliance with this Court's Order and the federal pleading standards. As such, the Court concludes repleading would be futile.

IV. CONCLUSION

For the foregoing reasons, Defendants' Motions to Dismiss...are GRANTED....

Notes and Questions

1. ***Upheld on Appeal***: The U.S. Court of Appeals for the Eleventh Circuit affirmed the district court's decision in *Halstead*.[12]

2. ***Concurring Opinion***: In a similar case, the complaint was short, but its sentences weren't. The court dismissed the plaintiff's complaint (but allowed a chance to amend) because the defendants couldn't possibly respond to its confusing allegations, which were "full of run-on sentences":

    > Plaintiff argues his Complaint satisfies the requirements of Fed. R. Civ. P. 8 because, in its entirety, it is relatively short. But this is not the governing standard. Rather, the Court must decide whether the pleading puts Defendants on notice of Plaintiff's allegations and allows them adequate opportunity to respond. *See Koll*, 397 F.2d at 126–27. The pleading here misses the mark, particularly on the "adequate opportunity to respond" prong. Many paragraphs (like those identified above) are long, confusing, redundant, and full of run-on sentences that mix factual allegations with editorial asides. They also often intermix allegations about the specific circumstances of Plaintiff's case with broadside allegations about how the University of Iowa "constantly" or "universally" or "routinely" handles investigations into alleged sexual misconduct. Defendants cannot reasonably be expected to respond to these allegations in their current form. *See, e.g., Mangan v. Weinberger*, 848 F.2d 909, 911 (8th Cir. 1988) (affirming dismissal of complaint that was "unreasonably verbose, confusing, and conclusory"); *Michaelis v. Neb. State Bar Ass'n*, 717 F.2d 437, 438–39 (8th Cir. 1983) (affirming dismissal of complaint that was "needlessly long, repetitious and confused"). The Court therefore GRANTS the motion to dismiss without prejudice and with leave to amend.[13]

3. ***Why Wordiness?*** As noted in this book's Foreword, we've avoided cases in which pro se litigants authored flawed pleadings (or

12. Halstead v. Espinoza, 2023 WL 2399288 (11th Cir. Mar. 8, 2023).

13. Doe v. Univ. of Iowa, 2022 WL 4182196, at *3 (S.D. Iowa Sept. 2, 2022).

other documents). The principal cases in this and other chapters involved lawyer-penned documents. Knowing that, and knowing that lawyers are supposed to be aware of and follow the controlling court rules, what accounts for pleadings that are decidedly *not* short, plain, and direct? Why do some lawyers ignore the rules' express, explicit call for direct, plain language?

C. In Statutes

Legislators are notorious for their heavy use of run-on sentences, making life difficult for lawyers and judges trying to determine legislative intent. Consider one poor judge who had to tame a statute "consist[ing] of a single run-on sentence of more than 250 words."[14] In his effort to capture the statute's meaning, he was forced to tabulate it within his opinion, much like a law student working on a classroom exercise.[15]

The Maine Supreme Court was once divided on the intended meaning of a statutory definition that "consist[ed] of a single, seventy-seven word run-on sentence that contain[ed] thirteen commas and employ[ed] the disjunctive 'or' eight times."[16] The Court's majority settled on an interpretation that alarmed the Maine Legislature, which moved swiftly to undo the Court's decision. Acknowledging that "there may be confusion in the application of the existing statutory definition," the legislature declared "an emergency within the meaning of the Constitution of Maine," requiring new legislation "immediately."[17] The legislature then amended the definition by tabulating it into a vertical list of numbered and lettered subparts.[18] Although the legislature did not explicitly own up to its carelessness in drafting the original version, its emergency

14. Roberts v. Crowley, 538 F. Supp. 2d 413, 418 n.6 (D. Mass. 2008).

15. *Id.* at 418–19.

16. Whitney v. Wal-Mart Stores, Inc., 895 A.2d 309, 318–19 (Me. 2006) (Levy, J., dissenting), *superseded by statute*, 5 Me. Rev. Stat. Ann. §4553-A; *see also* Me. Legis. Serv., ch. 385, Legis. Doc. 1027, Sen. Paper 344, 123d Leg., 1st Reg. Sess. (June 21, 2007).

17. Emergency preamble to 5 Me. Rev. Stat. Ann. §4553-A, contained in Me. Legis. Serv., ch. 385, Legis. Doc. 1027, Sen. Paper 344, 123d Leg., 1st Reg. Sess. (June 21, 2007).

18. *See* 5 Me. Rev. Stat. Ann. §4553-A.

amendment tacitly confirmed one justice's quip that the original run-on provision was "not a model of legislative clarity."[19]

Congress has likewise flummoxed courts with run-on sentences. And in the case below, the resulting ambiguity led to an overturned criminal conviction:

United States v. Ashurov

726 F.3d 395 (3d Cir. 2013)

FUENTES, Circuit Judge:

. . . .

Ashurov was originally charged with violating 18 U.S.C. §1546(a) by "knowingly making under oath" a materially false statement in the Forms I–20, but, given that he did not therein certify anything under oath, a superseding indictment was returned charging him only with "knowingly presenting a false statement." 18 U.S.C. §1546(a). A jury convicted him of one count, based on the April 2010 form, but the District Court granted him a judgment of acquittal, concluding that the oath requirement applied to both the "knowingly makes" and "knowingly presents" clauses and that, alternatively, it would apply the rule of lenity. The Government now appeals.

II. ANALYSIS

. . . .

At issue is the fourth paragraph of 18 U.S.C. §1546(a), which punishes:

> Whoever **knowingly makes under oath,** or as permitted under penalty of perjury under section 1746 of title 28, United States Code, knowingly subscribes as true, any false statement with respect to a material fact in any application, affidavit, or other document required by the immigration laws or regulations prescribed thereunder, or **knowingly presents** any such application, affidavit, or other document which contains any **such** false statement or which fails to contain any reasonable basis in law or fact.

(emphasis added [by the court]).

19. *Whitney*, 895 A.2d at 318 (Levy, J., dissenting).

Specifically, Ashurov was indicted for violating the "knowingly presents" portion of the statute. The question in this case is what exactly that clause proscribes.

....

We recognize and reiterate that the "rule of lenity requires more than a difficult interpretative question." *United States v. Flemming*, 617 F.3d 252, 270 (3d Cir. 2010). On the other hand, the idea embodied by the rule is that "the citizen is entitled to fair notice of what sort of conduct may give rise to punishment." *McNally v. United States*, 483 U.S. 350, 375, 107 S.Ct. 2875, 97 L.Ed.2d 292 (1987) (Stevens, J., dissenting). In this case, Congress has written a needlessly convoluted statute—a run-on sentence that is but one of four paragraphs contained in a single subclause of §1546. The sentence consists of 76 words and seven uses of the conjunction "or," and has a complicated history of amendments accompanied by nary an explanation—and carries stiff penalties at that (up to 10 years for run-of-the mill violations but as much as 25 years for some). We have labored through the meandering words of this law and carefully considered the well-presented arguments of both sides, and are still left with grievous doubt as to the statute's meaning. The statute thus falls well short of providing the required fair notice as to what it punishes. Accordingly, we apply the rule of lenity and decline to relax the "knowingly presents" crime of §1546(a) by removing from it the oath requirement that appears in the "knowingly makes" crime. "If Congress desires to go further, it must speak more clearly than it has." *Id.* at 360, 107 S.Ct. 2875 (Majority Op.). In the alternative, the Government is free to amend Form I–20 to require an oath from the applicants who complete it.

III. CONCLUSION

For the foregoing reasons, the District Court's judgment is affirmed.

■ ■ ■

Run-on sentences sometimes infect even the explanatory comments that are designed to help judges and lawyers unearth a statute's intended meaning. Consider one jurisprudential saga in which federal and state courts looked to a statute's explanatory comment for help, only to be confounded by an incomprehensible run-on sentence. The case, *Horton v. Alexander* (below), was a complex one involving alleged fraud by corporate insiders. Just before filing bankruptcy, a family-owned corporation transferred over $200,000 of corporate money to pay off family members' personal debts. During the bankruptcy case, the corporation's unsecured creditors tried to use Alabama's Fraudulent Transfer Act to get that money back from the recipients so that it would be available to creditors.

The creditors' case hinged on how the court interpreted the Act's "good-faith transferee" provision. That provision protects good-faith transferees who, in exchange for receiving a payment from the bankruptcy debtor, give some value to the debtor "or to another person." But what does "or to another person" mean? The United States District Court struggled with this question and, as you'll see, got no relief from the statute's explanatory comment:

Horton v. Alexander

2006 WL 3742175 (M.D. Ala. Dec. 18, 2006)

W. HAROLD ALBRITTON, Senior United States District Judge.

....

No case law exists explaining the rationale for the additional "or to another person" language in §8-9A-8(d). There is a Comment [footnote omitted] accompanying this statute that attempts to explain the significance of the additional language. It must be noted, however, that this Comment is poorly drafted, or poorly transcribed and edited, thereby providing little insight into what was the intent of the legislature. The Comment states that:

> This language is merely to clarify the fact that a good faith transferee is protected to the extent of value given by the transferee to one other than the debtor is effectively a transfer for the debtor to the one who receives the value, this transfer may under proper circumstances be a fraudulent transfer.

As one can easily see, this Comment makes little sense as written. It is a run-on sentence, leaving out a subject that could significantly alter the overall meaning of the language. Thus, the Comment creates confusion as opposed to answering any questions....

The interpretation of Ala.Code §8-9A-8(d) is critical in determining the liability, if any, of the transferees in this case. It is a question of state law of first impression, has far-reaching effect, and ultimately is unclear.... Therefore, considering the uncertainty of the relevant state law, the court finds that the appropriate action is to certify [the] question regarding the interpretation of §8-9A-8(d) to the Supreme Court of Alabama.

■ ■ ■

After agreeing to consider the certified question, the Alabama Supreme Court likewise looked to the Act's explanatory comment for help—only to suffer the same frustration as the federal court:

Horton v. Alexander

977 So. 2d 462 (Ala. 2007)

LYONS, Justice

This Court is asked to construe §8-9A-8(d), which reads as follows:

> "Notwithstanding voidability of a transfer under this chapter, a good-faith transferee is entitled, to the extent of the value given the debtor for the transfer *or to another person* as a consequence of the debtor's making such transfer, to
>
> > "(1) A lien on or a right to retain any interest in the asset transferred; or
> >
> > "(2) A reduction in the amount of the liability on the judgment."

(Emphasis added.)

Because we are dealing with the Uniform Fraudulent Transfer Act ("the UFTA"), we could ordinarily find persuasive authority from other jurisdictions construing similar language. However, that simple solution is unavailable because the emphasized language set forth above is unique to Alabama. Ordinarily in such a situation we would look to the Alabama Comment for an explanation of the reason for the deviation from the model act. However, nothing about this statute is ordinary.

The applicable portion of the Alabama Comment states:

> "3. The language, 'or to another person as a consequence of the debtor's making such transfer[,] to' is added to the Uniform Act in subsection

(d) of this section. This language is merely to clarify the fact that a good faith transferee is protected to extent of value given by the transferee to one other than the debtor is effectively a transfer for the debtor to the one who receives the value, this transfer may under proper circumstances be a fraudulent transfer...."

The second sentence begins with a tantalizing introductory phrase that suggests that clarification will follow, but the sentence then breaks down into an incomprehensible juxtaposition of unintelligible phrases.

[U]nder what we consider to be the plain meaning of the exception in §8-9A-8(d), a transferee acting in good faith under circumstances by which the transfer of the debtor's assets confers value on a person other than the transferee will be able to avoid repayment. Further, although the Alabama Comment can perhaps be charitably described as ambiguous, it cannot trump an unambiguous statute.

[W]e are unable to conclude that §8-9A-8(d), affording expanded relief to a good-faith transferee, apparently at odds with the general purpose of the Act, reaches an absurd result wholly beyond the reasonable contemplation of the legislature.... Any dissatisfaction with the consequences of the plain meaning of §8-9A-8(d) is a matter for the legislature.

Notes and Questions

1. *No Relief in Sight*: As of this writing, the Alabama Legislature has not amended its Fraudulent Transfer Act to clarify the provision at issue in *Horton*. The Alabama explanatory comment also remains unchanged—even though two courts have called it an "unintelligible" run-on sentence that "makes little sense as written."
2. *Cost of Confusion*: Would a careful edit of the Alabama explanatory comment have spared the *Horton* parties thousands of dollars in legal fees? Let's be conservative and assume a $200 hourly rate for each party's attorney. Let's also assume that each party's attorney spent at least 20 hours researching and briefing the issue for the bankruptcy court, 10 more hours doing the same for the United States District Court, and 20 more hours for the Alabama Supreme Court. Using these figures, the fees for researching and briefing this issue would have been at least $10,000 per party. This figure doesn't include fees for the lawyers' time spent preparing for and making

oral arguments in the three courts. Surely that would be another 15 hours. And it doesn't include the parties' out-of-pocket costs.

3. ***Dismissal***: In *Stanard v. Nygren*,[20] the Seventh Circuit affirmed a district court's refusal to allow a second amended complaint when the proposed complaint was "next to impossible" to decipher. Along with being verbose and riddled with grammatical, punctuation, and spelling errors, the proposed complaint contained more than 20 sentences with 100 or more words, including sentences of 291, 345, and 385 words.
4. ***The Pros Know—Short Is Strong***: The most accomplished legal writers, including many federal appellate judges, embrace short sentences. Consider this passage by Justice Elena Kagan:

   > Ford is a global auto company. It is incorporated and headquartered in Michigan. But its business is everywhere. Ford markets, sells, and services its products across the United States and overseas. In this country alone, the company annually distributes over 2.5 million new cars, trucks, and SUVs to over 3,200 licensed dealerships.[21]

   Three of those five sentences had fewer than eight words. Another was just thirteen words. Bryan Garner shows the same confidence with short sentences in this passage:

   > You may think that's just hyperbole. Sadly, it isn't. True enough, there may not be such a thing as a "pure describer," since every commentator has at least some predilections about usage, however covert. But many describers also dogmatically oppose value judgments about language. That in itself is a value judgment—and a very odd one, in the eyes of ordinary people.[22]

   Three of those five sentences had ten or fewer words. The other two were relatively long, lending a nice variety to the mix.

---

20. 658 F.3d 792, 799–800 (7th Cir. 2011).

21. Ford Motor Co. v. Montana Eighth Judicial Dist. Ct., 141 S. Ct. 1017, 1022 (2021).

22. Bryan A. Garner, *Making Peace in the Language Wars*, 7 Green Bag 2d 227, 229 (2004).

You'll notice the same style from accomplished authors of non-legal works. Consider this paragraph by late Nobel laureate Toni Morrison:

> Reading and script writing were prized in my family not only for information and pleasure but also as a defiant political act since historically so much effort had been used to keep us from learning. My mother joined the Literary Guild in the Forties. We subscribed to newspapers devoted exclusively to African-American news and opinions. Issues of the Pittsburgh Courier and the Cleveland Call and Post were worn to shreds with multiple readings and readers. Like other ethnic newspapers, ours elicited passionate commentary, questions, argument. We pored over JA Rogers's work, Du Bois's *The Souls of Black Folk* and whatever else we could find that encouraged and informed us about being black in America.[23]

Morrison's first sentence is 35 words. The rest are 9, 11, 20, 10, and 29 words. It's a rich variety, with 50% at 11 words or fewer.

So while working on your next draft, strive for sentence-length variety. And remember: short is strong.

5. ***AI Edit***: Generative artificial intelligence can help lawyers manage sentence length. Consider the following AI-assisted revision. For the original, we've selected a real statutory provision. It consists of a single 140-word sentence that leads into a vertical list. That long lead-in contains a general rule, the conditions for that rule's application, and an exception:

Original

> (1) Unless an act or omission is the result of gross negligence or willful misconduct, the acts or omissions of a medical first responder, emergency medical technician, emergency medical technician specialist, paramedic, medical

23. Toni Morrison, *Can We Find Paradise on Earth?*, The Telegraph (May 27, 2014, 9:00 a.m.), https://www.telegraph.co.uk/culture/hay-festival/10848569/Toni-Morrison-can-we-find-paradise-on-Earth.html.

> director of a medical control authority or his or her designee, or, subject to subsection (5), an individual acting as a clinical preceptor of a department-approved education program sponsor while providing services to a patient outside a hospital, in a hospital before transferring patient care to hospital personnel, or in a clinical setting that are consistent with the individual's licensure or additional training required by the medical control authority including, but not limited to, services described in subsection (2), or consistent with an approved procedure for that particular education program do not impose liability in the treatment of a patient on those individuals or any of the following persons:
>
> (a) The authorizing physician or physician's designee.
>
> (b) The medical director and individuals serving on the governing board, advisory body, or committee of the medical control authority and an employee of the medical control authority....

Again, that provision is a 140-word sentence that leads into a vertical list. The main subject and verb are 118 words apart. And it contains multiple series, some with potentially ambiguous modifiers. One series item is itself a series. In short, it is hardly a model of clarity. Let's see if AI can help.

Prompt to AI

Our prompt to ChatGPT was to "[r]edraft the following statute to avoid long, complicated sentences. Use short sentences and plain language. Here it is: [inserted provision]."

Below is what that prompt produced.

AI After Version

> (1) The acts or omissions of certain medical professionals while providing services to a patient do not create liability, unless they were grossly negligent or intentionally acted wrongfully. These professionals include medical first responders, emergency

> medical technicians, emergency medical technician specialists, paramedics, medical directors of medical control authorities or their designees, and clinical preceptors of department-approved education program sponsors (subject to subsection 5). The services they provide may be outside a hospital, in a hospital before transferring patient care, or in a clinical setting. These services should align with their licensure or additional training required by the medical control authority, or an approved procedure for the education program. This immunity from liability extends to the following individuals:
>
> > (a) The physician who authorized the medical professionals or their designee. (b) The medical director, members of the governing board, advisory body, or committee of the medical control authority, and employees of the medical control authority.

This revised version used five sentences before the list instead of one. It's still complicated, but it's a marked improvement. Some human editorial work, including informative headings and subheadings, would further improve it. And, as always, a lawyer–editor would need to research the substantive law to ensure accuracy.

D. Exercise

The sentence below is grammatically correct and has proper punctuation. Yet it rambles. Revise it by breaking it into multiple sentences:

> Even on its own terms, it is unclear what the school district's argument proves because either interpretation of §1415(*l*) operates to preclude some unexhausted claims, and under our view, for example, a plaintiff who files an ADA action seeking both damages and the sort of equitable relief IDEA provides may find his request for equitable relief barred or deferred if he has yet to exhaust §1415(f) and (g), so it is "quite mistaken to assume," too, that any interpretation of a law that does more to advance a statute's putative goal "must be the law."

After you're finished, check *Luna Perez v. Sturgis Public Schools*, 598 U.S. 142, 150 (2023).

EIGHT

Comma Mistakes Can Slow Climate Talks and Cost Millions

A. Overview

For a punctuation mark that's just a speck, the comma has caused lots of trouble—sometimes for being inserted where it should *not* be and sometimes for not being inserted where it *should* be. One comma caused the 2007 United Nations Climate Change Conference to devolve into a debate that has continued for years.[1] The controversy concerned participating countries' obligations under the Bali Action Plan.[2] The Plan described mitigation obligations in two paragraphs, one for *developed* countries and the other for *developing* countries. But the paragraphs' wording and punctuation didn't match, creating ambiguity.[3]

1. Susan Biniaz, *Comma but Differentiated Responsibilities: Punctuation and 30 Other Ways Negotiators Have Resolved Issues in the International Climate Change Regime*, 6 MICH. J. ENV'T & ADMIN. L. 37, 46–47 (2016); Bloomberg, *"Famous Comma" Slows Climate Talks*, ECON. TIMES (Dec. 18, 2009), https://economictimes.indiatimes.com/famous-comma-slows-climate-talks/articleshow/5349749.cms.

2. Biniaz, *supra* note 1, at 46–47.

3. *Id.* at 47.

The paragraph for developed countries described

> [m]easurable, reportable and verifiable nationally appropriate mitigation commitments or actions, including quantified emission limitation and reduction objectives...."[4]

But the paragraph for developing countries described

> [n]ationally appropriate mitigation actions by developing country Parties in the context of sustainable development, supported and enabled by technology, financing and capacity building, in a measurable, reportable and verifiable manner...."[5]

Despite the missing Oxford comma, the first paragraph made clear that developed countries must take actions that are "measurable, reportable and verifiable." In the developing-country paragraph, however, those same adjectives might refer to either the "nationally appropriate mitigation actions" or the "technology, financing and capacity building" support available to developing countries. Some developing countries argued for the latter interpretation—that the "measurable, reportable and verifiable" requirement did not apply to the mitigation actions themselves but only to the *support* for those mitigation actions. They argued that developing countries' actions should not be subject to verification unless the countries received support in the form of technology, funding, or capacity building.[6]

The troublesome comma was the one after "capacity building." The United States insisted on the comma to help ensure that "actions" by developing countries—not just support from industrialized nations—would be "measurable, reportable and verifiable."[7] In other words, the comma was meant to protect against the very disagreement that occurred—and that raged for hours as nearly 200 countries argued about how the paragraph impacted each group's responsibilities for cutting greenhouse-gas emissions.[8] The debate caused Qua-

4. U.N. Framework Convention on Climate Change, Conf. of the Parties, *Report of the Conference of the Parties on Its Thirteenth Session, Held in Bali from 3 to 15 December 2007 Addendum Part Two: Action Taken by the Conference of the Parties at Its Thirteenth Session*, U.N. Doc. FCCC/CP/2007/6/Add.1, at 3 (March 14, 2008), https://unfccc.int/resource/docs/2007/cop13/eng/06a01.pdf.

5. *Id.*

6. Biniaz, *supra* note 1, at 47.

7. Bloomberg, *supra* note 1.

8. Biniaz, *supra* note 1.

mrul Chowdhury, the Bangladeshi envoy who'd been negotiating climate issues since 1992, to comment: "One comma creates a lot of trouble."[9]

And in case you question this provision's importance, two years later when the nations met again in Copenhagen, U.S. Senator John Kerry said that when it comes to what the United States wants from China, verification is the "single most important ingredient."[10] Even two years after that, the comma was still a point of serious debate among the parties.

B. The $5 Million (Missing) Comma

Beyond impacting international climate change, commas have sparked litigation (and made headlines) right here in the United States. In the case below, it was the absence, not the presence, of a comma that sparked debate—and that cost an employer millions of dollars.

The missing comma was the so-called serial or Oxford comma. It's been referred to as "the most polarizing of punctuation marks."[11] A serial comma typically appears before an "and" or "or" that sets off the last item in a series of three or more. For example, if you say that your favorite classes are Contracts, Torts, and Civil Procedure, the comma after "Torts" is the serial comma.

Legal writers should use the serial comma to avoid potential ambiguity.[12] How can omitting it create ambiguity? Take this sentence:

- I'm going to invite my cousin, a singer and a composer.

How many people were invited? One talented cousin who sings and composes? Three people—a cousin, another person who is a singer, and a third person who is a composer? Or two people—a cousin who sings and someone else who composes? Inserting the serial comma clarifies the meaning: *I'm going to invite my cousin, a singer, and a composer.*

Another example:

- My favorite people are my parents, Wonder Woman and Superman.

---

9. Bloomberg, *supra* note 1.

10. *Id.*

11. LYNN TRUSS, EATS, SHOOTS & LEAVES 84 (2003).

12. *E.g.*, DIANA J. SIMON, THE (NOT TOO SERIOUS) GRAMMAR, PUNCTUATION, AND STYLE GUIDE TO LEGAL WRITING (2022); BRYAN A. GARNER, THE REDBOOK: A MANUAL ON LEGAL STYLE 4 (4th ed. 2018).

Without a comma after Wonder Woman, this sentence suggests that Wonder Woman and Superman are the author's parents—highly unlikely. Placing a serial comma after Wonder Woman would resolve the ambiguity: *My favorite people are my parents, Wonder Woman, and Superman.*

The lack of this clarifying serial comma gave rise to the newsworthy outcome in *O'Connor v. Oakhurst Dairy.*[13] The issue there was whether an employer was required to pay its employees overtime under a Maine statute providing for wage and overtime payments. The court held that the employer owed the overtime pay, and the employer ended up settling the case for $5 million.[14]

O'Connor v. Oakhurst Dairy

851 F.3d 69 (1st Cir. 2017)

BARRON, Circuit Judge.

For want of a comma, we have this case. It arises from a dispute between a Maine dairy company and its delivery drivers, and it concerns the scope of an exemption from Maine's overtime law. Specifically, if that exemption used a serial comma to mark off the last of the activities that it lists, then the exemption would clearly encompass an activity that the drivers perform. And, in that event, the drivers would plainly fall within the exemption and thus outside the overtime law's protection. But, as it happens, there is no serial comma to be found in the exemption's list of activities, thus leading to this dispute over whether the drivers fall within the exemption from the overtime law or not.

....

[The court explained that, under Maine's wage and hour laws, employees must be paid overtime. The statute defined "employee" broadly, but the definition excluded a few categories of workers. At issue in this case was Exemption F.]

....

Exemption F covers employees whose work involves the handling—in one way or another—of certain, expressly enumerated food products. Specifically, Exemption F states that the protection of the overtime law does not apply to:

---

13. 851 F.3d 69 (1st Cir. 2017).

14. John McCoy, *Oakhurst Dairy's $5M Settlement Driven by Grammar Rules*, Bloomberg L. News (Feb. 9, 2018), https://news.bloomberglaw.com/daily-labor-report/oakhurst-dairys-5m-settlement-driven-by-grammar-rules.

The canning, processing, preserving, freezing, drying, marketing, storing, packing for shipment or distribution of:

1. Agricultural produce;
2. Meat and fish products; and
3. Perishable foods.

The parties' dispute concerns the meaning of the words "packing for shipment or distribution."

The delivery drivers contend that, in combination, these words refer to the single activity of "packing," whether the "packing" is for "shipment" or for "distribution." The drivers further contend that, although they do handle perishable foods, they do not engage in "packing" them. As a result, the drivers argue that, as employees who fall outside Exemption F, the Maine overtime law protects them.

[The employer] responds that the disputed words actually refer to two distinct exempt activities, with the first being "packing for shipment" and the second being "distribution." And because the delivery drivers do—quite obviously—engage in the "distribution" of dairy products, which are "perishable foods," [the employer] contends that the drivers fall within Exemption F and thus outside the overtime law's protection.

The delivery drivers lost this interpretive dispute below.... The delivery drivers now appeal that ruling. They raise a single legal question: what does the contested phrase in Exemption F mean?

Each party recognizes that, by its bare terms, Exemption F raises questions as to its scope, largely due to the fact that no comma precedes the words "or distribution." But each side also contends that the exemption's text has a latent clarity, at least after one applies various interpretive aids. Each side then goes on to argue that the overtime law's evident purpose and legislative history confirms its preferred reading.

[The employer] argues that, when we account for these canons here, it is clear that the exemption identifies "distribution" as a stand-alone, exempt activity rather than as an activity that merely modifies the stand-alone, exempt activity of "packing."

[The employer] acknowledges that its reading would be beyond dispute if a comma preceded the word "distribution" and that no comma is there. But, [the employer] contends, that comma is missing for good reason. [The employer] points out that the Maine Legislative Drafting Manual expressly instructs that: "when drafting Maine law or rules, don't use a comma between the penultimate and the last item of a series." In fact, [the employer] notes, Maine statutes invariably omit the serial comma from lists.[15] And this practice reflects a drafting convention that is at least as old as the Maine wage and hour law, even if the drafting manual itself is of more recent vintage....

[The delivery drivers] acknowledge that the drafting manual advises drafters not to use serial commas to set off the final item in a list—despite the clarity that the inclusion of serial commas would often seem to bring. But the drivers point out that the drafting manual is not dogmatic on that point. The manual also contains a proviso—"Be careful if an item in the series is modified"—and then sets out several examples of how lists with modified or otherwise complex terms should be written to avoid the ambiguity that a missing serial comma would otherwise create.

Thus, the drafting manual's seeming—and, from a judge's point of view, entirely welcome—distaste for ambiguous lists does suggest a reason to doubt [the employer's] insistence that the missing comma casts no doubt on its preferred reading. For, as the drivers explain, the drafting manual cannot be read to instruct that the comma should have been omitted here if "distribution" was intended to be the last item in the list. In that event, the serial comma's omission would give rise to just the sort of ambiguity that the manual warns drafters not to create.

The text has, to be candid, not gotten us very far. We are reluctant to conclude from the text alone that the legislature clearly chose to deploy the nonstandard grammatical device of asyndeton. But we are also reluctant to overlook the seemingly anomalous violation of the parallel usage canon that [the employer's] reading of the text produces. And so—there being no comma in place to break the tie—the text turns out to be no clearer on close inspection than it first appeared. As a result, we turn to the parties' arguments about the exemption's purpose and the legislative history. [The court found that evidence of purpose and history did not point to a result either way. But based on the policy of construing wage and hour laws liberally to protect employees, the court held that the employees were entitled to overtime.]

....

15. Authors' note: In a footnote, the court pointed out that it would be "remiss not to note the clarifying virtues of serial commas that other jurisdictions recognize." 851 F.3d at 75 n.5.

Notes and Questions

1. *Neglected Pets (and Punctuation)*: Assume that a person failed to provide medical care for a cat. As a result, the cat suffered unnecessary physical pain. The person was charged under a statute that imposes criminal liability for neglecting an animal. Specifically, one key part of the law provides that a person "who deprives any animal of necessary sustenance, food or drink" is guilty of a misdemeanor. The defendant argued that because of the absence of a serial comma after "food," the word "sustenance" only included food or drink and did not include medical care. The court, commenting on the law's grammatical construction, stated that, had the legislature intended to list three separate types of deprivation, the statute would have read "sustenance, food, or drink." As an example, it referenced an author's dedication "to my parents, the Pope and Mother Theresa," pointing out that the absence of the serial comma created ambiguity. Do you think that the defendant prevailed?[16]

C. No Comma Means No Comma (Perhaps)

In the next case, the court also refused to ignore a comma's absence, enforcing the statute as written. As you read, ask yourself whether you side with the trial court (which believed that the missing comma was an obvious typo) or the appellate court (which didn't):

Village of West Jefferson v. Cammelleri

2015 WL 3824456 (Ohio App. 2015)

ROBERT ALLEN HENDRICKSON, J.

Defendant-appellant, Andrea Cammelleri, appeals from a decision of the Madison County Municipal Court finding her guilty of violating a parking time limit ordinance. For the reasons outlined below, the judgment of the trial

16. *See* People v. Walsh, 859 N.Y.S.2d 906 (Crim. Ct. 2008).

court is reversed, Cammelleri's conviction is vacated, and Cammelleri is discharged.

At approximately 5:30 p.m. on February 13, 2014, Cammelleri had just woken up after working third shift when she looked out her window and noticed her pickup truck was no longer parked on the street in front of her house. Thinking her pickup truck had been stolen, Cammelleri called 911. The dispatcher inquired as to the make and model of Cammelleri's vehicle and told Cammelleri that her pickup truck had not been stolen, but had been impounded. A police officer later went to Cammelleri's house and gave her the parking citation.

Cammelleri was cited for violating West Jefferson Codified Ordinances 351.16(a), which states:

> It shall be unlawful for any person ... to park ... upon any street ... in the Village, any motor vehicle camper, trailer, farm implement and/or non-motorized vehicle for a continued period of twenty-four hours....

Cammelleri contested the citation, and on March 18, 2014, the matter proceeded to a bench trial. At trial, Cammelleri stipulated that her 1993 Ford pickup truck was parked on the street outside of her house located in West Jefferson in excess of 24 hours. The only issue was whether the ordinance actually applied to Cammelleri's pickup truck. Cammelleri argued the ordinance did not apply because the language prohibits a motor vehicle camper [and not a motor vehicle] from being parked on the street for an extended period of time. The village contended the ordinance did apply because a comma was inadvertently omitted between the phrase "motor vehicle" and the word "camper."

The trial court held that when reading the ordinance in context, it unambiguously applied to motor vehicles and "anybody reading [the ordinance] would understand that it is just missing a comma." The trial court then found Cammelleri guilty of violating West Jefferson Codified Ordinances 351.16(a) and ordered her to pay court costs.

In her first assignment of error, Cammelleri argues the trial court erred in finding she violated West Jefferson Codified Ordinances 351.16(a) by parking her pickup truck on the street in front of her house in excess of the allotted time period because her pickup truck was not subject to the ordinance. More specifically, Cammelleri argues her pickup truck does not constitute a motor vehicle camper as identified by the ordinance. By using the phrase "motor vehicle camper," Cammelleri asserts the ordinance specifically identified and prohibited a camper that is propelled by an engine from parking on the street in excess of 24 hours. In contrast, the village argues it is clear a comma is missing between the phrase "motor vehicle" and the word "camper," and thus, the ordinance applies to Cammelleri's pickup truck as a motor vehicle. We agree with Cammelleri.

In this instance, the intent of the ordinance is plain from the grammar and language used in West Jefferson Codified Ordinances 351.16(a). According to ordinary grammar rules, items in a series are normally separated by commas. The items included in the series of motor vehicle camper, trailer, and farm implement are separated by commas. In order to interpret the ordinance in the way the village suggests, prohibiting parking either a motor vehicle or a camper upon a street in the village for over 24 hours, a comma must be inserted between the phrase "motor vehicle" and the word "camper." However, no such comma exists. According to the rules of grammar, "motor vehicle camper" is one item.

By utilizing rules of grammar and employing the common meaning of terms, "motor vehicle camper" has a clear definition that does not produce an absurd result. If the village desires a different reading, it should amend the ordinance and insert a comma between the phrase "motor vehicle" and the word "camper." As written, however, legislative intent is clear from looking at the language used in the ordinance itself.

Applying the ordinance to the case at bar, Cammelleri's pickup truck does not meet the definition of "motor vehicle camper." While it is a motor vehicle, Cammelleri's pickup truck is not equipped for camping. Moreover, Cammelleri's pickup truck does not fall within the purview of other enumerated items in West Jefferson Codified Ordinances 351.16(a).

Consequently, the trial court erred in finding Cammelleri violated the ordinance by parking her pickup truck on the street in front of her house located in West Jefferson in excess of 24 hours. Cammelleri's first assignment of error is sustained.

Judgment reversed, Cammelleri's conviction is vacated, and Cammelleri is hereby discharged.

Notes and Questions

1. ***Legislative Drafting***: If village officials wanted to amend the statute discussed in *Village of West Jefferson* to apply to motor vehicles, golf carts, and motorized scooters, how could they amend the ordinance to reflect that? (By the way, did you know that some lawyers devote their careers to legislative drafting? Rather than working on

cases, they work for the state or federal government writing laws. Or they might work for a private firm but draft ordinances for a municipal client.)

2. ***Comma Conflict***: Let's assume that a husband and wife have separated and signed a Separation Agreement. The Separation Agreement provides as follows: "The parties acknowledge that should they divorce, Wife shall be entitled to one-half of Husband's retirement, 401K or other employment benefits." Based on this provision and a missing serial comma after 401K, the wife argues that she is entitled to either one-half of her husband's retirement *and* 401K *or* one-half of his other employment benefits. Alternatively, she argues that the three words in the list—retirement, 401K, and other—all modify the term "employment benefits," entitling her to one-half of all employment benefits, whether that includes retirement, 401K, or other such benefits. In contrast, the husband argues that this language means the wife can only pick one of the three types of benefits. How would you rule on this issue and why?[17]

3. ***The Haze of Horizontal Lists***: Let's assume you wanted a settlement agreement to bind two parties in a case—call them Party A and Party B—and their respective heirs, devisees, legatees, personal representatives, and agents. Begin with the words, "This agreement binds. . . ." How would you draft the provision to ensure that it binds everyone?[18]

   Might a plain drafting style eliminate or greatly reduce the import of commas and canons? Do we always need exhaustive horizontal lists, which are prone to ambiguity arising from modifiers and punctuation choices? Revisit the plain-language release in Chapter 3. How did its drafter handle this challenge?

17. *See* Christian v. Christian, 794 S.E.2d 51 (Ga. 2016).

18. See *Daniel v. Hawkins*, 289 A.3d 631 (Del. 2023), especially the discussion at page 666.

D. Commas and Canons

The next two cases are challenging. Both show courts looking to canons of construction to resolve ambiguity—and both courts considered whether the absence of a comma impacted whether or how those canons should apply.

As mentioned in a previous chapter, canons of construction are interpretive conventions (or presumptions) meant to aid courts in resolving ambiguity. The "last antecedent" canon, for example, purports to clarify whether modifying language that trails a series applies to *all* the series items or to just the *last item*. For instance, in the sentence below, does the modifying phrase "with brown fur" apply to just the hamster or to *all* the listed pets?

- You may choose a purebred show dog, a house cat, or a hamster with brown fur.

Under the last-antecedent canon, courts would generally presume that the trailing modifier ("with brown fur") modifies only the final series item ("a hamster"). So you're free to choose a dog or a cat with any color fur.

But some courts and commentators believe that the presence of a comma between the final series item and the modifier turns this canon on its head, signaling that the trailing modifier applies to *all* the series items:

- You may choose a purebred show dog, a house cat, or a hamster, with brown fur.

If a court accepts this comma exception, then any pet you choose must have brown fur, whether it's a dog, a cat, or a hamster.

Note that there isn't universal agreement over the merits of these (and other) canons. And as you read the next case, you'll sense the court's discomfort with relying on a canon or its exception to discern legislative intent. The case involved a mother who sought to modify her daughters' parenting schedule after she moved. The applicable statute was ambiguous about whether the mother had to show that her move made the current parenting plan impractical. A commissioner held that it did, and the mother appealed. The Washington Court of Appeals began its opinion with an unusual epigraph: two quotations speaking to the court's frustration over the missing comma that might have clarified the trailing modifier's reach:

In re Marriage of Cardwell

479 P.3d 1188 (Wash. App. 2021)

FEARING, J.

> *If such was the intent of the legislature, the grammar used defeated that purpose. This concurrence is written to bring this specific situation to the attention of the legislature and to suggest the desirability of adding a grammarian to their technical staff.* In re Estate of Kurtzman, *65 Wash.2d 260, 269, 396 P.2d 786 (1964) (Hill, J., concurring).*
>
> *No one knows when and when not to use a comma.* Kay Brossard, Washington State comma expert.

The mother of two daughters, Regan Cardwell, appeals denial of her request for a minor modification of the girls' residential schedule after her change in domicile returned her to the children's home city. The appeal requires us to enter a wonderland of grammatical conventions in order to construe an ambiguous statute addressing the grounds on which a parent may gain a minor modification. We decline to apply the ostensible last antecedent rule and interpret the controlling statute, RCW 26.09.260(5)(b), to require that a parent who moves residences must show that the current schedule is impractical in order to procure a modification. We agree with the trial court that the mother failed in her showing.

....

RCW 26.09.260 controls the modification of a parenting plan. The language of RCW 26.09.260, consistent with the Uniform Marriage and Divorce Act, establishes a strong presumption against modification and in favor of continuity....

[In pertinent part, the statute provides that:]

> (5) The court may order adjustments to the residential aspects of a parenting plan *upon a showing of a substantial change in circumstances of either parent* or of the child, and without consideration of the factors set forth in subsection (2) of this section, if the proposed modification is *only a minor modification in the residential schedule that does not change the residence the child is scheduled to reside in the majority of the time and*:
>
> ....

(b) Is based on a change of residence of the parent with whom the child does not reside the majority of the time or an involuntary change in work schedule by a parent which makes the residential schedule in the parenting plan impractical to follow.

....

The poor drafting of RCW 26.09.260(5)(b) creates the ambiguity of whether the phrase "which makes the residential schedule in the parenting plan impractical to follow" at the end of the subsection applies to both the clauses "a change of residence of the [nonresidential] parent" and "an involuntary change in work schedule by a [nonresidential] parent" or only the latter of the two clauses. We label the phrase "which makes the residential schedule in the parenting plan impractical to follow" as the modifying or qualifying phrase. We brand the two preceding phrases as antecedents. A "change in work schedule" is the last antecedent. Note that no comma follows the second usage of "parent" at the end of the second or last antecedent and before the word "which," which begins the modifying clause.

....

Washington courts employ the last antecedent rule in cases of statutory interpretation. Under this rule, qualifying or modifying words and phrases refer to the last antecedent. A corollary principle is that the presence of a comma before the qualifying phrase evidences that the qualifier is intended to apply to all antecedents instead of only the immediately preceding one. Use of a comma therefore looms important, and RCW 26.09.260(5)(b) lacks this punctuation mark. Therefore, the last antecedent rule indicates that the disputed phrase in RCW 26.09.260(5)(b) should only modify "involuntary change in work schedule" and not "change in residence."

We must choose whether to follow the last antecedent rule. Courts need not always strictly adhere to technical grammatical rules in interpreting statutory provisions. The last antecedent rule is one of many aids to discovery of intent or meaning, but is not inflexible and uniformly binding. The rule of the last antecedent can be overcome by other indicia of meaning. A court may even abandon the rule despite it offering a sensible result.

Although we lack authority to abrogate the last antecedent rule, we question its validity. All written language needs some invented grammar rules for effective communication, but the English language lacks any final arbiter of the rules. History suggests that courts manufactured the last antecedent rule for purposes of contract and statute interpretation rather than grammarians creating the rule antecedent to court rulings....

We conclude that the legislature requires a substantial change in circumstance and also a showing that the residential schedule in the parenting plan is impractical for a change in residence and an involuntary change in work schedule.

....

■ ■ ■

In the next case, *ECB USA, Inc. v. Chubb Insurance Co.*,[19] the plaintiffs urged a similar result. They argued that because the telltale "exception" comma was absent, the last-antecedent canon dictated that the trailing modifier applied to only the final series item.

But the insurer answered back with its own canon: the series-qualifier canon. The series-qualifier canon holds that if there is a straightforward, parallel series of nouns or verbs ("car, truck, or motorcycle"), a modifier that comes before or after that series applies to *every* series item: *A car, truck, or motorcycle licensed with the State.* The *ECB* court adopted this interpretation.

As you will see, the *ECB* case highlights the potential for tension between competing canons. Note also that unlike the court in *Oakhurst Dairy*, which gave interpretive weight to a serial comma's absence, the *ECB* court said that a drafter's use of a post-series clarifying comma is "discretionary":

ECB USA, Inc. v. Chubb Insurance Co.

587 F. Supp. 3d 1165 (S.D. Fla. 2022)

ROBERT N. SCOLA, JR., United States District Judge

[The defendant insurance companies filed a motion for summary judgment, and the plaintiffs, who were suing because the insurance companies refused to defend them in a separate lawsuit referred to as "the Underlying Lawsuit," filed a cross-motion for summary judgment.]

....

19. 587 F. Supp. 3d 1165 (S.D. Fla. 2022).

As a general matter, insurance policies and insurance salesmen have long been the butt of jokes. The former are not known for beautiful prose nor the latter for exciting conversation. But insurance contracts can provide fodder for scores of attorneys, grammarians, and logophiles, where, as here, the meaning of one phrase and the placement (or omission) of one comma can make the difference between coverage and nothing....

In relevant part, the 2017–18 Policy provided coverage for claims related to "Management consulting services," which are defined as "services directed toward expertise in banking finance, accounting, risk and systems analysis, design and implementation, asset recovery and strategy planning for financial institutions."

....

[T]he Underlying Lawsuit did not concern the provision of accounting services to a "financial institution." This is undisputed. The Plaintiffs' only argument in opposition comes down to a comma. Recall the clause at issue: "[1] services directed toward expertise [2] in banking finance, accounting, risk and systems analysis, design and implementation, asset recovery and strategy planning [3] for financial institutions."

The Defendants argue that covered accounting services must be provided to a financial institution, pointing to the series-qualifier canon, which holds that a modifier (here, "for financial institutions") at the end of a series of nouns or verbs "normally applies to the entire series." The Plaintiffs argue that the series-qualifier canon only applies where there is a comma before the modifier—therefore, as there is no comma before "for financial institutions," the Plaintiffs argue that clause only qualifies the phrase immediately preceding it (namely, "asset recovery and strategy planning").

The Court finds that the phrase "for financial institutions" modifies the entire series, meaning that "management consulting services" is defined as the provision of "services directed towards expertise in... accounting... for financial institutions." *See United States v. Bass*, 404 U.S. 336, 340 n.6, 92 S.Ct. 515, 30 L.Ed.2d 488 (1971) (noting that while "commas at the end of series can avoid ambiguity," the "use of such commas is discretionary").

In total, a plain reading of the 2017–18 Policy establishes that [the insurance company] had no duty to defend or duty to indemnify in connection with the Underlying [Lawsuit], as the services at issue in the Underlying [Lawsuit] were not provided to a financial institution, as required for coverage. Therefore, the Court grants summary judgment in favor of [the insurance company]....

....

Notes and Questions

1. ***Fair Fees?*** A plaintiff sued a defendant for defamation and lost. Texas law provided that the prevailing party could recover attorney's fees and other expenses. Accordingly, the defendant requested some $67,000 in attorney fees and some $4,000 in costs. After a hearing, however, the court announced that "justice and equity" necessitated reducing the defendant's recovery in fees to only $6,500 and costs to only $1,500. Unhappy with these reduced amounts, the defendant appealed. The law in question provided as follows: "If the court orders dismissal of a legal action under this chapter, the court shall award to the moving party: (1) court costs, reasonable attorney's fees, and other expenses incurred in defending against the legal action as justice and equity may require...." The defendant argued that he should have received all attorneys' fees because the phrase "as justice and equity may require" only modified "other expenses" and not the phrase "reasonable attorney's fees." Specifically, the defendant argued that if the legislature had intended for attorney's fees to be adjusted based on equity and justice, it would have eliminated the serial comma after "attorney's fees." Do you think the defendant prevailed?[20]

E. Common Comma Issues (and How to Navigate Them)

This casebook isn't meant to replace reference manuals on usage, grammar, and punctuation. But we see value in clarifying some comma rules that get heavy use in everyday legal writing. If lawyers misfire on these rules, they jeopardize clarity.

1. Commas in Compound Sentences

Insert a comma before a coordinating conjunction (*for*, *and*, *nor*, *but*, *or*, *yet*, *so*) that joins two complete sentences. The resulting product is what grammarians call a "compound sentence." This is because the sentence actually contains two sentences (or "independent clauses"), which are connected by the conjunction.

20. *See* Sullivan v. Abraham, 488 S.W.3d 294 (Tex. 2016).

The comma before the conjunction helps busy readers process this grammatical structure and prevents the sentence from taking on a rambling quality.

Take this sentence:

- My legal-writing professor wants us to turn papers in using Word, but I always forget and turn in a PDF.

The comma after *Word* is the comma triggered by the coordinating conjunction *but*, which joins two complete sentences. Note how the comma enhances readability.

Here are two more examples, both from Chief Justice John Roberts's opinion in the 2023 *Moore v. Harper* decision:

- *Smiley* did not endorse such murky inquiries into the nature of constitutional restraints, <u>and</u> we see no neat distinction today.
- *Marbury* proclaimed our authority to invalidate laws that violate the Federal Constitution, <u>but</u> it did not fashion this concept out of whole cloth.

Notice in each example how the clauses on either side of the conjunction each have their own subject and verb—and could stand alone independently.

2. Avoiding Comma Splices

What happens when you try to join two complete sentences with a comma but *without* the coordinating conjunction? You end up with a "comma splice," which is improper.[21] It's called a comma splice because the comma is being used to "splice together two complete sentences when that isn't the function of a comma."[22]

Here's an example of what *not* to do:

- I walked my dog in the park, he loved chasing the ducks.

The comma after *park* is a comma splice. The author has spliced together two complete sentences with just that comma. But it's an easy fix with many options:

---

21. SIMON, *supra* note 12, at 9–17.

22. MIGNON FOGARTY, GRAMMAR GIRL'S QUICK AND DIRTY TIPS FOR BETTER WRITING 104 (2008). *See also* GARNER, *supra* note 12, at 5 ("Don't join independent clauses with a comma alone. Grammarians consider that construction, called a *comma splice*, a form of run-on sentence.").

1. Replace the comma with a period. (I walked my dog in the park. He loved chasing the ducks.)
2. Replace the comma with a semicolon. (I walked my dog in the park; he loved chasing the ducks.)
3. Add a coordinating conjunction after the comma. (I walked my dog in the park, and he loved chasing the ducks.)
4. Use an em-dash instead of a comma. (I walked my dog in the park—he loved chasing the ducks.)

3. Setting Off Extra Stuff

Reference manuals list a dizzying number of comma rules, some of which blur or overlap: *use a comma or commas to set off introductory phrases, to set off introductory clauses, to set off nonrestrictive clauses, to set off nonrestrictive appositives, to set off parenthetical phrases, to set off nonrestrictive relative clauses, to set off sentence-starting dependent clauses, to set off participial phrases*... and on and on. Only the most ardent punctuation enthusiast can avoid a sense of intimidation.

It's empowering to learn comma rules by name. But it's also helpful to remember that every rule listed above (and more that we haven't listed) are really the *same* comma rule: the extra-stuff rule. In other words, use a comma or commas to set off extra stuff.

What does this mean? Well, let's start with a sentence, meaning an independent clause that states the writer's core idea. Here's one from Chief Justice John Roberts, again from the *Moore* opinion:

- The record before us shows that *Harper I* "finally decided" the Elections Clause issue.

That sentence is fine as is. But if Chief Justice Roberts wished to add something more to this core idea, that new information (extra stuff) might show up at the start, in the middle, or at the end of the sentence—or in multiple places. As it happens, in *Moore* he chose to add extra stuff at the start and at the end. We'll underline that extra stuff so that you can track it easily and see where his commas set it off:

- <u>In short</u>, the record before us shows that *Harper I* "finally decided" the Elections Clause issue, <u>which has survived subsequent proceed-</u>

ings in the North Carolina Supreme Court such that it continues to "require decision" by this Court.

You see that the original independent clause remained unchanged. He simply added extra stuff at the start (a short introductory phrase) and at the end (a long nonrestrictive clause).

In the next sentence, Chief Justice Roberts added extra stuff in the middle of the sentence, so he used commas on *both sides* to set it off. Again, we're underlining the extra stuff so that you can track it easily:

- James Iredell, who would later serve as an inaugural Justice of this Court, penned at the time an open letter "To the Public" expounding a robust concept of judicial review.

Typically, it's not ideal to separate the sentence's subject (James Iredell) from its verb (penned). But here, the interruption is short, and it works quite well.

Be on the lookout for the words *who* and *which*. They often (but not always) signal extra stuff that needs to be set off.

A final point: Whenever you begin a sentence with *although*, *because*, or *if*, that creates a sentence-starting dependent clause (introductory extra stuff) that draws a comma. Again from Chief Justice Roberts:

- Although judicial review emerged cautiously, it matured throughout the founding era.

F. Exercises

Review the sentences below and identify any comma splices:

1. My sister's name is Francine, her favorite color is blue.
2. Fifty-six people attended the party, my nemesis and I were the first people to arrive.
3. I lost my case; my client was unhappy with the verdict, I should have worked harder to achieve a better outcome.
4. The professor cold-called me, I didn't know the answer but made something up, obviously my answer was wrong and I was embarrassed about it, but the professor didn't give me a hard time about it; I was relieved that she let me off the hook.

Identify whether any of the sentences below are missing serial commas. If they are, identify the possible interpretations of each sentence that could have been resolved by including a serial comma:

1. My neighbor was accosted by two dogs, a boxer and a shepherd.
2. The strawberries we picked were bright and fragrant and delicious.
3. I am going to invite my friend, a comic and an athlete over to watch the Super Bowl.
4. My professor was interviewed about his forthcoming article, "Criminal Law Monthly Reporting," and his research and writing habits.

The following sentences all have so-called extra stuff added to the independent clause. Where should the commas go? If it helps, identify the main subject and verb, and then underline the core grammatical sentence. Then insert a comma or commas to set off the extra stuff:

1. My neighbor an electrical engineer was accosted by two dogs.
2. After the lunch meeting we picked strawberries and put them in a basket which became quite heavy.
3. Because I've invited more than 30 people to the party I am buying extra potato chips and hot dogs.
4. The judge who was growing frustrated held me in contempt citing my "failure to observe appropriate courtroom decorum."
5. The red Chevy a real throwback to muscle-car days roared down Main Street.

Instead of commas, might you try em-dashes or parentheses in any of the above sentences? Commas are the neutral choice. Em-dashes tend to emphasize—adding a bit more swagger or structure. And parentheses tend to deemphasize (in most situations).

NINE

Semicolons and the Secession of West Virginia

A. Overview

The semicolon is an odd duck. It's not a period, which indicates a full stop, and it's not a comma, which indicates more of a pause. It's a hybrid—weaker than a period but stronger than a comma. And perhaps because it is strange and unique, writers have given it many interesting nicknames, such as the "king comma,"[1] the "soft period,"[2] "the great mediator,"[3] "the yellow light in a New York sentence,"[4] and a "chimera with its 'colon head and comma tail.'"[5]

---

1. Bryan A. Garner, The Redbook: A Manual on Legal Style 15 (4th ed. 2018).

2. Anne Enquist, *The Semicolon's Undeserved Mystique*, 12 Perspectives: Teaching Legal Res. & Writing 105, 105 (2004).

3. Kelley Lonergan, *The Semicolon: A Love Story*, Thought Catalog (Feb. 18, 2014), https://thoughtcatalog.com/kelley-lonergan/2014/02/the-semicolon-a-love-story/.

4. Sam Roberts, *Celebrating the Semicolon in a Most Unlikely Location*, N.Y. Times (Feb. 18, 2008), https://www.nytimes.com/2008/02/18/nyregion/18semicolon.html.

5. Cecelia Watson, *Nine Things You Didn't Know About the Semicolon*, Millions (July 29, 2019), https://themillions.com/2019/07/9-things-you-didnt-know-about-the-semicolon.html.

Two primary semicolon rules appear in modern style guides. The first is that if a period is correct, then a semicolon is also correct—as a style choice emphasizing the two sentences' closely related subject matter: *Rex was overcome by excitement; he bolted straight toward the ducks.* The second is to replace serial commas with semicolons in a complex series—usually meaning a series in which one or more items have internal punctuation: *The court ordered supplemental briefs, which are due in one week; an amended notice of hearing; and a joint appendix of exhibits.*[6] Note that these rules are for traditional prose. When it comes to outlines, vertical lists, and the like, all bets are off.

Semicolons have been in use for more than 500 years,[7] so they're nothing new. The Framers of our Constitution used semicolons frequently—the original Constitution contains roughly 65 semicolons.[8] In fact, scholars have written about one semicolon in our Constitution that calls into question whether West Virginia was lawfully formed as a state back in 1863. The story of how West Virginia became a state goes back to the Civil War.[9]

When the Civil War broke out, the territory that today is West Virginia was part of Virginia. Virginia refused to fight against other southern states and seceded after President Lincoln called for the states to enlist soldiers in the Union army following the Battle of Fort Sumter. Less than a month after Virginia seceded, pro-Union Virginians voted to form a second government, the Restored Government of Virginia. In August, the Restored Government of Virginia voted to approve the creation of a new state, West Virginia—in

---

6. You'll also find a rule calling for a semicolon before a conjunctive adverb that joins two independent clauses. (*We told Rex to stay; however, he bolted as soon as he saw the ducks.*). But that's the same as our first rule. A period would work there, so a semicolon works, too.

7. Melissa Gouty, *The Fascinating History of the Controversial Semicolon*, Writing Cooperative (Jan. 17, 2020), https://writingcooperative.com/the-fascinating-history-of-the-controversial-semicolon-c13918316df2.

8. In case you are thinking that the Framers of our Constitution did not care about punctuation, that assumption is incorrect. In fact, the Framers created a "Committee of Style and Arrangement" to handle punctuation, capitalization, and similar matters. Vasan Kesavan & Michael Stokes Paulsen, *Is West Virginia Unconstitutional?*, 90 Calif. L. Rev. 291, 334, 337–38 (2002).

9. The information in this section is drawn from a number of sources: Kesavan & Paulsen, *supra* note 8; Nat'l Archives Ctr. for Leg. Archives, *West Virginia Statehood, June 20, 1863* (July 26, 2019), https://www.archives.gov/legislative/features/west-virginia; and Adam Shelton, *The Article IV, Section III Controversy*, Inst. for Just. (May 8, 2020), https://ij.org/cje-post/the-article-iv-section-iii-controversy/.

essence, seceding from secessionist Virginia. The secessionist Virginia government did not consent. Congress approved creation of the new state and passed a West Virginia statehood bill in 1862, which Lincoln signed. Because Lincoln believed secession was illegal, he accepted that Virginia had consented through its restored government, despite the secessionist government's lack of consent.

Was this constitutional? The answer turns on a semicolon.

The applicable constitutional provision is Article IV, Section 3, and buried between two semicolons is a prohibition against states being formed "within the Jurisdiction of any other State":

> New States may be admitted by the Congress into this Union; but no new State shall be formed or erected within the Jurisdiction of any other State; nor any State be formed by the Junction of two or more States, or Parts of States, without the Consent of the Legislatures of the States concerned as well as of the Congress.

The second semicolon creates ambiguity because it is unclear whether the phrase "without the Consent of the Legislatures of the States concerned as well as of the Congress" applies to both states formed "within the Jurisdiction of any other State" and "by the Junction of two or more States, or Parts of States. . . ." If the consent clause applies, new states can be created "within the Jurisdiction of" existing states if the state legislature(s) and Congress consent. But if not, the Constitution seemingly prohibits new states from being created this way.

Simply put, whether West Virginia is a constitutionally created state depends on whether the second semicolon is acting more like a period or a comma.

Does that mean there can never be a breakaway state created by splitting the territory of an existing state, period? Even though a state can be formed from parts of other states if the states "concerned" and Congress consent? Or is the semicolon acting more like a comma, meaning that an individual state can cleave into two states if the existing state and Congress consent?

Here, even assuming Virginia could constitutionally split into two states, West Virginia's constitutionality remains uncertain because of the secondary issue of Virginia's consent. Could either the secessionist or Reformed governments of Virginia consent if seceding meant Virginia was no longer a "state" under the Constitution? If Virginia could still claim statehood, which government had the legitimate power to consent? While these are interesting questions, they can be left for another day because West Virginia's statehood is settled. West Virginians do not walk around worried that they might be living in a state that is not constitutional. In this case, politics outweighed punctuation.

But that doesn't mean people were unaware that the semicolon created ambiguity. They were. For proof, look no further than justices of the Supreme Court. When quoting the ambiguous constitutional provision, many writers simply replaced the semicolons with commas or periods. For example, in his *Commentaries on the Constitution*, Justice Story misquoted the provision by replacing the first semicolon with a period and the second with a comma.[10] Similarly, in three Supreme Court cases quoting the provision, the Court artfully replaced the second semicolon with a comma, effectively circumventing the ambiguity in the actual text.[11]

Interestingly, if West Virginia is unconstitutional, it's in good company—Vermont, Kentucky, Tennessee, and Maine would also be unconstitutional because these states also formed by breaking off from existing states. Fortunately, no one is questioning whether these states were lawfully formed because of a semicolon. But, as demonstrated below, semicolons continue to stir up trouble because their presence creates ambiguities that require interpretation.

B. In Statutes and Regulations

The first case below concerned runny, unpasteurized eggs. Because the yolks were too soft and undercooked, inspectors at a nursing home determined that the eggs could lead to serious illness. The government argued that the facility violated a safety regulation requiring that food be served in a sanitary manner. Fortunately, no one got sick. But an ambiguous semicolon gave the court a headache, forcing it to interpret unclear guidelines on how to cook unpasteurized eggs:

---

10. 2 Joseph Story, Commentaries on the Constitution of the United States 195, §1314 (Melville M. Bigelow, ed., 5th ed., William S. Hein & Co., Inc. 1994) (1891).

11. Pollard v. Hagan, 44 U.S. (3 How.) 212, 223 (1845); Dred Scott v. Sanford, 60 U.S. (17 How.) 393, 500 (1856); Coyle v. Smith, 221 U.S. 559, 566 (1911).

Elgin Nursing & Rehabilitation Center v. U.S. Department of Health & Human Services

718 F.3d 488 (5th Cir. 2013)

SMITH, Judge.

[While investigating Elgin, a residential care facility, State inspectors found two plates with egg yolk "smeared around the plate." Investigators interviewed residents and the kitchen manager, who confirmed that five residents had asked for soft-cooked, unpasteurized eggs. The State concluded that unpasteurized shell eggs, when served soft-cooked, could cause serious illness or death, and found that Elgin was out of compliance with a regulation requiring facilities to serve food in a "sanitary" manner.]

....

[The] requirement in the Code of Federal Regulations, however, is somewhat vague—"sanitary conditions" requires further specification. Thus [the Department of Health and Human Services] fashioned guidelines interpreting and clarifying the regulation. The [guidelines are codified in an interpretive manual], which provides:

Final Cooking Temperatures

> Cooking is a critical control point in preventing foodborne illness. Cooking to heat all parts of food to the temperature and for the time specified below will either kill dangerous organisms or inactivate them sufficiently so that there is little risk to the resident if the food is eaten promptly after cooking. Monitoring the food's internal temperature for 15 seconds determines when microorganisms can no longer survive and food is safe for consumption. Foods should reach the following internal temperatures: ...
>
> Unpasteurized eggs when cooked to order in response to resident request and to be eaten promptly after cooking;—145 degrees F for 15 seconds; until the white is completely set and the yolk is congealed.

[T]here are potentially dueling requirements regarding temperature and consistency of the egg. [The government] appears to interpret the [manual] as imposing a conjunctive requirement; that is, the egg must be cooked at 145°F., *and* the white must be completely congealed and the yolk firm.

....

The [manual's] directive is inherently ambiguous.... There are [] two possible requisites: (1) time and temperature and (2) degree or extent of congealing. [The government's] proposed interpretation treats that phrase as conjunctive—absence of either is a violation. Elgin proposes that the phrase is disjunctive—meeting either is sufficient.

The language and context of the [manual] show that a disjunctive reading is the better. The punctuation between the clauses—a semicolon—tends to suggest related but separate ideas and stands for "or," not "and." Clauses separated by a semicolon are presumed to be independent clauses.... That does not establish whether the clauses are conjunctive or disjunctive, however. Moreover, punctuation alone is not "a reliable guide for discovery of a statute's meaning."

The canon of construction that all clauses be given effect strongly recommends a disjunctive reading. If the two phrases are read conjunctively, one will be rendered effectively meaningless. As was demonstrated by [a food-safety instructor's] video and affidavit, an egg may be cooked for 15 seconds at 145°F. but still have a runny yolk. If the regulation were read conjunctively—requiring both the stated cooking time and the prescribed level of consistency—the former requirement would be nullified; the egg would always have to be cooked until the yolk hardened, and the time requirement would never matter.

Considering the specific instructions regarding eggs in the context of the [manual] as a whole also points to a disjunctive reading. The title of the relevant... subsection is "Final Cooking Temperatures," which suggests that the times and temperatures are the primary focus. The egg-preparation instructions are part of a list of other food preparation instructions; for example, "Fish and other meats—145 degrees F for 15 seconds." Every other food-preparation direction includes only a temperature and time.

The fact that a consistency-and-appearance requirement is attached to eggs alone suggests that there is something different about them, and indeed there is. It is possible to take the internal temperature of meat while it is cooking and verify that it remains at that temperature for a certain period of time. An egg's temperature may also be taken if it is cooked in certain ways. It is impossible, however, to take an egg's internal temperature while it is being boiled—thus some other metric is required to ensure safe cooking.

Consistency and appearance together serve as such a proxy. Thus, an egg must be either cooked at 145° F. for 15 seconds or cooked until the white is set and the yolk congealed; either alternative is sufficient. Such a reading fits best within the context of the regulation and gives full meaning to all its parts.

....

Because the [manual] is disjunctive, [the government] was required to adduce evidence that eggs were not cooked at the correct temperature for the proper amount of time; absent such evidence, it could not establish that Elgin had failed to satisfy that requirement. [The government] presented no evidence regarding temperature, cooking time, or cooking method of the eggs in question.

. . . .

Notes and Questions

1. *Meta Semicolons?* Did you notice the *Elgin* court's own semicolons? We've selected (and cleaned up) some sentences from the opinion that included properly placed semicolons. Notice that in each example, a complete sentence appears on both sides of the semicolon, which replaces the terminal period that we'd typically see there:
   - If the regulation were read conjunctively, the former requirement would be nullified; the egg would always have to be cooked until the yolk hardened, and the time requirement would never matter.
   - The government appears to interpret the manual as imposing a conjunctive requirement; that is, the egg must be cooked at 145°F., and the white must be completely congealed and the yolk firm.
   - Because the manual is disjunctive, the government was required to adduce evidence that eggs were not cooked at the correct temperature for the proper amount of time; absent such evidence, it could not establish that Elgin had failed to satisfy that requirement.
2. *Clam Challenge*: Assume that you're drafting a regulation for cooking clams safely. Normally, clams should be steamed in hot water for four to six minutes. But another way to tell whether they're fully cooked is that their shells pop open. If the shells do not pop open after steaming them, they are rotten and should be discarded. Draft a regulation to ensure that clams are prepared in a safe manner. Experiment with semicolons as you work. Do they always threaten clarity, or might their careful, correct use help?

In the next case, employees of a managed-care organization sued their former employer, alleging that it had failed to pay them overtime required by the Fair Labor Standards Act. The employer, a nonprofit organization, claimed that the Wisconsin Administrative Code, which used a semicolon in defining the words "commercial establishment," didn't apply, so the suit should be dismissed. Notice how the disputed language roughly mimics what we see in some dictionaries, with alternative definitions—usually short fragments—separated by semicolons. That style would dictate a disjunctive "or" reading.

Paczkowski v. My Choice Family Care, Inc.

384 F. Supp. 3d 991 (W.D. Wis. 2019)

STEPHEN L. CROCKER, Magistrate Judge

Plaintiff Katy Paczkowski brings this action on behalf of herself and all other similarly situated employees, as a collective and class action against her former employer, defendant My Choice Family Care, Inc. ("My Choice"), for violations of the Fair Labor Standards Act... and Wisconsin wage and hour laws. Paczkowski is a former Care Manager at My Choice, a non-profit managed care organization. In this suit, Paczkowski contends that My Choice violated the FLSA and Wisconsin law by failing to pay overtime compensation to her and other Care Managers.

Before the court is My Choice's motion to dismiss Paczkowski's state law claim on the ground that My Choice is a nonprofit organization to which Wisconsin's overtime regulation... does not apply. Paczkowski does not dispute My Choice's nonprofit status but disagrees with its contention that nonprofits generally are not covered by Wisconsin's overtime regulation. Because I agree that the terms of the regulation do not apply to My Choice, I am granting My Choice's motion for partial dismissal.

....

By its terms, [the regulation at issue] applies only to [an enumerated list of types of employers, including] mercantile establishments.... The parties agree that the only term in this regulation that might apply to My Choice is "mercantile establishment." "Mercantile" happens to be one of only five defined terms in [the regulation], but as discussed below, [the Wisconsin Department of Workforce Development's (DWD)] definition is so turbid that it defies unequivocal exegesis. According to DWD's rules, "mercantile" means "pertaining to merchants or trade," and is synonymous with the word commercial.

....

DWD's definition gets clumsier as it progresses, which provides plaintiff with an[] opportunity to argue that My Choice is a "commercial" establishment. Plaintiff points out that [DWD] defines "commercial" as follows:

> Commercial is viewed with regard to profit or designed for profit; designed for mass appeal, emphasizing skill and subjects useful in business.

Focusing on the semicolon, plaintiff notes that "[a] semicolon is most commonly used to link (in a single sentence) two independent clauses that are closely related in thought." . . . From this, plaintiff argues that by using a semicolon in this sentence, [DWD] meant to designate two alternate scenarios in which an establishment will be deemed "commercial":

1. when it is "viewed with regard to profit or designed for profit"; or
2. when it is "designed for mass appeal, emphasizing skill and subjects useful in business."

Further, plaintiff argues, if the second clause is not given independent meaning, then it is mere surplusage.

Plaintiff's argument has some traction. Notably, by contrast, DWD defines "trade" with a series of phrases separated by semicolons; there, it is plain that the semicolons function as disjunctive "ors," with each phrase setting out alternative meanings of the word "trade," as one would find in a dictionary. No reasonable argument can be made that in the sentence defining "trade" the semicolons function as "ands." If they did, then the sentence would make no sense. Next, it would be illogical to contend that DWD used semicolons as "ands" when defining "commercial," but then switched them to "ors" when it defined trade. Thus, I agree with plaintiff that by using a semicolon before the phrase "designed for mass appeal, emphasizing skill and subjects useful in business," the agency intended to describe a separate meaning of the word "commercial."

[Even though the court agreed with the plaintiff on how the clause should be construed, the resulting meaning was still ambiguous. The court applied other interpretive guidelines and concluded that My Choice, as a nonprofit, was not subject to Wisconsin's overtime laws. The court granted the motion to dismiss but gave the plaintiff leave to amend the complaint.]

■ ■ ■

A semicolon also created a fuss in an immigration law that authorized the Secretary of Labor to deport certain noncitizens. The statute, which used two semicolons, provided as follows:

> At any time within five years after entry, any alien who at the time of entry was a member of one or more classes excluded by law;... any alien who was convicted, or who admits the commission, prior to entry, of a felony or other crime of misdemeanor involving moral turpitude;... shall, upon the warrant of the Secretary of Labor, be taken into custody and deported.[12]

Based on this wording, what if a citizen of another country is convicted of a felony before arriving in the United States, but the United States doesn't initiate deportation proceedings until more than five years after that person's entry? Does the five-year time frame apply or not?

In the case below, the noncitizen argued that it applied to all the listed scenarios, including the prior-conviction scenario. The court disagreed, finding that the five-year limitation applied to only the statute's first clause, not the rest. But the court did so only after a thorough analysis of the semicolon. (This is one of our few historical cases. Be on the lookout for word choices that betray its age, including one word that has drawn much scrutiny—and disfavor—in recent decades.)

McLeod v. Nagle

48 F.2d 189 (9th Cir. 1931)

SAWTELLE, Circuit Judge.

[This appeal is by a British citizen who entered the United States in 1924. A few months before he entered, he was convicted of breaking and entering in Vancouver, British Columbia. The United States instituted deportation proceedings in April 1930, more than five years after his entry. The British citizen argues that the deportation order was void because the United States didn't act within five years after his entry.]

....

12. Pillisz v. Smith, 46 F.2d 769, 770 (7th Cir. 1931) (quoting 8 U.S.C. §155 (1926)). The full text of the statute is quite lengthy, so only the pertinent portions have been included even though the court did evaluate the entire statute in interpreting it.

Crowell's Dictionary of English Grammar . . . says: "The semicolon is used to separate independent clauses that are not joined by a conjunction as 'He cried; I laughed'; to separate co-ordinate clauses of unusual length and those that contain commas, whether or not the clauses are joined by conjunctions; to separate conditional clauses joined by conjunctive adverbs." The clauses of the instant section are each as independent as the clauses of the example given, because of the fact that, although the predicate is expressed only once for the sake of brevity, it is elliptical to each of the sections set off by semicolons[.]

Again, Ward's "Sentence and Theme" says the semicolon "shows that two sentences, each of which should stand alone, have been combined into one sentence"; and continues, "A semicolon is used to show that what follows is grammatically independent, though closely related in thought."

From the point of view of strict grammatical construction, therefore, it is evident that, since the semicolon has been used to set off the various subdivisions of the section, the initial phrase, "within five years after entry," cannot be presumed to carry over into the subsequent clauses that are separated from the initial clause by a semicolon. The initial phrase, "within five years after entry," is set off by a comma, a weaker punctuation mark than the semicolon. The function of that comma is to set off the phrase from the rest of the clause in which it appears, and not from the rest of the entire section. The semicolon effectually isolates the opening clause and its dependent phrase from the other and subsequent clauses. These clauses have only one grammatical construction in common; they are joint subjects of the common predicate with which the entire section is brought to a close.

. . . .

It must . . . be conceded that [the appellant] also belongs to the special class for which no time limit is fixed. . . . Here Congress has expressly excepted aliens convicted of crime prior to their entry into the United States from the general classification of those who are excluded by law. The language is clear, and so to construe it gives each clause of section 19 its due importance; to construe it so that a five-year limitation would be attached to the clause in question would render void a definite statement of the will of Congress. [Therefore, we affirm the lower court's judgment that the appellant was lawfully deported.]

Notes and Questions

1. ***Semicolon Separation***: A (clumsy) city charter in Tennessee provides that the mayor "shall have the authority, subject to confirmation by the board, to make appointments, promotions and transfers of employees; to make demotions suspensions and removals of officers and employees for cause; and may delegate such authority as he deems advisable." The mayor wants to demote, suspend, and remove officers and employees (for cause) without the city council's or board's consent. Can the mayor do that?[13]

2. ***Stray Semicolon***: A driver's license was suspended for a year following the driver's conviction on a charge of careless and negligent driving resulting in death. This was his first offense. The driver appealed the suspension of his license, arguing that the maximum suspension was only 30 days, not 365 days. The applicable Vermont statute appears below. Note that the driver was convicted under §1091, so we've bolded that for you:

   > The suspension shall be a period of 10 days when an accumulation of 10 points, 30 days for 15 points, 90 days for 20 points and for a period increasing by 30 days for each additional 5 points; except the suspension period for a conviction for first offense of sections 674, **1091**, 1094, 1128, and 1133 of this title shall be 30 days; for a second conviction 90 days and for a third or subsequent six months, or the suspension period under the point values, whichever is greater, but if a fatality occurs, the suspension shall be for a period of one year.

   Did the driver prevail? Should the driver have prevailed?[14]

3. ***Semicolon Setback***: Landowners wanted to build a swimming pool on their lakefront property but to do so needed a zoning variance. Although the applicable ordinance required a 65-foot setback from the lake to build a pool, the landowners wanted this shortened to a 35-foot setback based on the shape of their lot and soil conditions.

---

13. *See* https://www.mtas.tennessee.edu/system/files/mrln/mknowledge/main/Use%20of%20Semi-Colon%20public_rev2017.pdf.

14. *See* Hill v. Conway, 463 A.2d 232 (Vt. 1983).

The ordinance stated that variances could only be granted in the situations below:

> 1. Where by reason of exceptional narrowness, shallowness or shape of a specific piece of property, which at the time of adoption of this chapter, was a lot or plat of record; or
>
> 2. Where, by reason of exceptional topographic conditions or other extraordinary or exceptional conditions of a piece of property, the strict application of the development requirements of this chapter would result in practical difficulties to, and undue hardship upon, the owner of this property, which difficulty or hardship is not the result of acts of the applicant; and further provided that this relief may be granted without substantially impairing the intent and purpose of this chapter and is not contrary to the public welfare.

The trial court concluded that subsection (1) incorporated the language of (2), so a variance could only be granted under (1) if subsection (2)'s hardship requirement was also satisfied. Therefore, the trial court upheld the county board's denial of the variance because the landowners had failed to prove hardship.[15]

4. ***Semicolons Go Global***: Semicolons have even impacted international law. After World War II, the Allied Powers signed the Nuremberg Charter.[16] It was prepared in French, English, and Russian, but the punctuation varied in the three languages. In Russian, the semicolon after the word "war" below was a comma, but the original French and English text inserted a semicolon instead:

   > CRIMES AGAINST HUMANITY: namely, murder, extermination, enslavement, deportation, and other inhumane acts committed against any civilian population, before or during the war; or persecutions on political, racial or religious grounds

---

15. *See* Sprayberry v. Bd. of Comm'rs of Putnam Cnty., 884 S.E.2d 429 (Ga. Ct. App. 2023).

16. Sean O'Reilly, *How a Semicolon Changed International Law*, MEDIUM (July 20, 2018), https://medium.com/@sean.patrick.oreilly96/how-a-semicolon-changed-international-law-292f012bc813.

> in the execution of or in connection with any crime within the jurisdiction of the Tribunal, whether or not in violation of the domestic law of the country where perpetrated.

The semicolon after the words "before or during the war" had profound implications for the tribunal's jurisdiction. Read literally, the second clause would expand the tribunal's jurisdiction to beyond the outbreak of World War II, *with no requirement* that the prosecution prove a connection to crimes against peace or war crimes.

The Allies did not want prosecutions for crimes that took place before the invasion of Poland, so they passed the "Protocol Rectifying Discrepancy in the Charter," which replaced Article 6(c)'s semicolon with a comma, to match the Russian text.[17]

5. ***The Semicolon Law***: A 1900 dispute between two Massachusetts men had far-reaching implications.[18] A man walked into a hotel shortly after 11 p.m., sat down at the bar, and ordered a drink. The hotel owner, who knew that the man had frequented a competitor hotel, refused to serve him. Yet the hotel owner continued to pour drinks for other customers. The man, incensed, hired a lawyer and sued the hotel owner for discriminating against him. The applicable liquor-sales statute said

> [t]hat no sale of spirituous or intoxicating liquor shall be made between the hours of 11 at night and 6 in the morning; nor during the Lord's day, except that if the licensee is also licensed as an Innholder he may supply such liquor to guests who have resorted to his house for food and lodging.

The lawyer, noting the statute's ambiguity, sought an injunction barring the hotel owner from serving anyone at all after 11 p.m. The local court granted the injunction. On appeal, the Mas-

17. *The Avalon Project, Nuremberg Trial Proceedings Vol. 1, Protocol Rectifying Discrepancy in the Charter*, Yale L. Sch., Lillian Goldman L. Libr. (last visited Apr. 10, 2023), https://avalon.law.yale.edu/imt/imtprot.asp.

18. The following is summarized from Cecelia Watson's excellent article, *Points of Contention: Rethinking the Past, Present, and Future of Punctuation*, 38 Critical Inquiry 649, 661–63 (Mar. 2012).

sachusetts Supreme Court upheld the injunction despite agreeing that the originally enacted statute used a comma in place of the semicolon. Because the version of the statute then in force used the semicolon and added the title "An Act to prohibit the sale of spirituous or intoxicating liquors between the hours of eleven at night and six in the morning," the Court concluded that the statute was meant to prohibit all alcohol sales between 11 p.m. and 6 a.m.

What followed was over six years of contention and, occasionally, outright chaos, as vividly recounted by author Cecelia Watson:

> Once the ruling came down, Boston police were ordered to begin enforcing the law strictly, and so they did, to the financial detriment of innkeepers. The innkeepers, along with everyone else with an interest in liquor sales, began organizing themselves in order to appeal to the state legislature on the first day of its session. Accordingly, a bill to amend what was now called the Semicolon Law came before the Massachusetts senate in April 1901, where members argued over the original intent of the legislature. After vigorous debate, a vote was taken, and the amended bill failed 21 to 10.
>
> The law continued to attract national attention and stir debate. In the Washington Post, Willard Holcomb wrote about the social ramifications of the dispute, which was now "well known throughout the country, owing to the great wailing and gnashing of teeth from this Commonwealth." Bostonians were not going to let "misfit commas and semicolons" hold them down, however, and they quickly found means by which to evade the law: if liquor was not to be sold after11 o'clock, they would simply order all they could before the cutoff, and then go on enjoying it afterwards at their leisure. This turned drinking into a kind of competitive sport: Bostonians would show up early at restaurants, stake out tables, and "order up the whole wine list." Those unfortunates who decided to go to the theater before dinner thus found it nearly impossible to find a seat in a restaurant afterwards; and if, against the odds, a seat could be found, its occupant would have to settle for "temperance drinks," since by that point, all the alcohol was sold out and making its way down the throats of people at neighboring tables. "The life of the latter-day Puritan," Holcomb concluded,

> "is not entirely devoid of alcoholic glee." But this glee was not quite Bacchanalian enough for opponents of the Semicolon Law; and for advocates of the law, it only served as a reminder of the depths to which Bostonians might sink if given full and free access to alcohol. The battle between the two camps roared vigorously on.[19]

Over the next few years, repeated attempts to repeal the Semicolon Law failed. In 1906, Massachusetts hotel owners and liquor dealers finally prevailed—at least partially. By seeking only a partial repeal, they convinced the legislature to extend the liquor-sales window by one hour, to midnight.

C. In Contracts

Semicolons have also sparked litigation in contracts cases. In the first case below, the court had to interpret an insurance policy's ambiguous semicolon. Specifically, the issue was whether the homeowner was entitled to coverage for property damage from a fire to a second home when the policy arguably only covered the policyholder's primary residence.

Lee v. Mercury Insurance Co. of Georgia

808 S.E.2d 116 (Ga. App. 2017)

SELF, Judge.

[The plaintiff regularly traveled between Georgia and Florida to work on projects in each place. After the plaintiff's childhood friend developed significant financial difficulties, the plaintiff agreed to purchase his friend's home in Georgia, but he allowed his friend to continue living there. He did, however, stay at the house a few nights each week when he was there for business. There was a house fire, and the issue is whether the insurance policy provided coverage for this second home.]

....

The policy defines "residence premises" as follows:

---

19. *Id.* at 662 (citations omitted).

> "**Residence premises**" means the one, two, three or four family dwelling, condominium or rental unit, other than structures and grounds, used principally as a private residence; where you reside and which is shown in the Declarations. (Emphasis in original).

....

Based upon the placement of the semicolon in the definition of "residence premises," a layperson could reasonably understand the defined term to mean "the one, two, three or four family dwelling, condominium or rental unit, other than structures and grounds, used principally as a private residence" *or* "where you reside and which is shown in the Declarations." Punctuation is an important indicator of meaning. The semicolon is normally employed in marking off a series of sentences or clauses of coordinate value, that is, to separate consecutive phrases or clauses which are independent of each other grammatically, but dependent alike on some word preceding or following. [Internal quotation marks omitted]. In this case, the definition of "residence premises" could be read by a layperson as having two separate, consecutive clauses (definitions) dependent alike upon the preceding word "means."

The dissent states that "the plain language" of the policy "provides that it covers the residence premises and defines such as a private residence where the insured resides." In order to reach this result, however, the dissent must rewrite the policy by removing the semicolon. This we cannot do. "It is the duty of the courts to construe and enforce contracts as made, and not to make them for the parties. The law will not make a contract for the parties which is different from the contract which was executed by them."

To support the claim that we should read the semicolon out of the policy, the dissent cites cases relying upon an anachronistic view of punctuation that are also factually distinguishable.... In *Bridges*, a case not involving the construction of an insurance policy, we cited the Century Dictionary as "'tell[ing] us, what is common knowledge, that 'there is still much uncertainty and arbitrariness in punctuation.'" We also cited law dating back to 1837. In their treatise on the proper interpretation of legal texts, Justice Scalia and Professor Garner explain why this historic bias against punctuation exists and should no longer be continued in modern times:

> No helpful aid to interpretation has historically received such dismissive treatment from the courts as punctuation—periods, semicolons, commas, parentheses, apostrophes. The original reason was understandable enough. Punctuation was considered of small account because it was

thought to be "the work of the engrossing clerk or the printer." And, again in days of yore, it was held that because many legislators voted only on the basis of bills that they heard read aloud—without seeing the printed page—they could take no notice of the punctuation marks....

....

Commentators have often said that "punctuation is never permitted to control, vary, or modify the plain and clear meaning of the language of the body of the act." This must be a remnant of the former denigration of punctuation that had not been adopted by the legislature; in modern times, we see no rational basis for such a rule. As is the case with other indications of meaning, the body of a legal instrument cannot be found to have a "clear meaning" without taking account of its punctuation. There is no reason to exclude punctuation from this stage of the inquiry. And we disagree with the position that the use of punctuation as an interpretive aid should be relied on only "when all other means fail."

Punctuation is often integral to the sense of written language....

As this is not a case in which an intent contrary to the punctuation used by the insurance company in drafting the policy plainly appears, we cannot ignore the semicolon. [We thus hold in the plaintiff's favor.]

■ ■ ■

The court's chief judge had very different views on the semicolon:

DILLARD, Chief Judge, concurring in part and dissenting in part.

The majority's Herculean effort to manufacture ambiguity out of otherwise unexceptionable and plain policy language is perfectly understandable. Lee is a sympathetic party. He stepped up to help a dear friend during a difficult time, and for that, we commend him. But the policy says what it says, and no act of kindness can change that. Nevertheless, the majority has chosen to disregard the plain meaning of the policy and well-settled precedent in order to achieve a result to its liking—accomplishing this extraordinary feat with only a semicolon....

....

[T]he majority argues that whether the policy language required Lee to reside at the home as a condition for coverage is at best ambiguous. And faced with the policy's plain language belying this contention, the majority conscripts the semicolon separating the term "private residence" and "where you reside" in the definition of "residence premises," and assigns it the disjunctive properties of the word "or." So tasked, the majority then asserts that the semicolon's placement could allow a layperson to understand "residence premises" to mean "the one, two, three or four family dwelling, condominium or rental unit, other structures and grounds, used principally as a private residence" *or* "where you reside and which is shown in the Declarations." Finally, the majority maintains that my reading of the "residence premises" definition, conjunctively rather than disjunctively, rewrites the policy by removing the semicolon.

In considering the majority's argument, I begin by acknowledging that, in some situations, "[p]unctuation is an important indicator of meaning." That said, the Supreme Court of the United States has rightly noted that it "will first take the instrument by its four corners, in order to ascertain its true meaning; if that is apparent, on judicially inspecting the whole, the punctuation will not be suffered to change it." Similarly, this Court has held that "[t]he punctuation of an instrument may be considered when the meaning is doubtful, but it cannot control if the meaning otherwise plainly appears." Indeed, punctuation is "always subordinate to the text, and is never allowed to control its meaning." Put simply, "the words control the punctuation marks, and not the punctuation marks the words."

Here, the majority argues that the placement of the semicolon *creates* ambiguity in the "residence premises" definition, thus burdening that punctuation mark with a laboring oar that, under our case law and common use, it was never meant to carry. Moreover, following the majority's grammatical logic to its necessary conclusion, if one construes the definition of residence premises disjunctively, the subject policy would provide coverage for "the one, two, three or four family dwelling, condominium or rental unit, other structures and grounds, used principally as a private residence" *without* any requirement that such dwelling be "shown in the Declarations." Suffice it to say, such a tortured reading would then put this definition at odds with the "Coverage" section of the policy, which as previously noted provides that Mercury covers "the dwelling on the residence premises *shown in the Declarations* used principally as a private residence...."

....

Moreover, even if I were inclined to assign the semicolon the level of import the majority claims it deserves, I disagree that it supports the result the majority reaches. As *The Chicago Manual of Style* explains, "[i]n regular prose, a semicolon is most commonly used between two independent clauses not joined by a conjunction to signal a *closer connection* between them than a period would." This description of the semicolon's most common use is echoed by *Garner's Modern American Usage*, which describes the semicolon as "a kind of supercomma" that "separates sentence parts that need a more distinct break than a comma can signal, but that are *too closely connected to be made into separate sentences....*" And these descriptions of the semicolon's most common use do not appear to be in conflict with the description offered by the majority—"[t]he semicolon is normally employed in marking off a series of sentences or clauses of coordinate value, that is, to separate consecutive phrases or clauses which are independent of each other grammatically, but dependent alike on some word preceding or following." It is simply baffling that the majority believes this language somehow justifies the insertion of an "or" in the definition of "residence premises" or disjunctive treatment of the independent clauses at issue. Given these particular circumstances, I find the majority's construction of the "residence premises" definition entirely unpersuasive. Accordingly, the trial court correctly concluded that the policy did not provide Lee with coverage and that Mercury was entitled to summary judgment on that ground.

■ ■ ■

Texas Supreme Court justices likewise locked horns over the meaning of a semicolon in a contract between an engineer and a developer with plans to convert a shopping center into condominium units.

Criswell v. European Crossroads Shopping Center, Ltd.

792 S.W.2d 945 (Tex. 1990)

HIGHTOWER, Justice.

....

Criswell is a registered engineer and surveyor. Ginsberg was general partner for Crossroads, a Texas limited partnership formed for the purpose of building a shopping center. Criswell was hired by Crossroads in 1970 to do the structural engineering for the center. After the center was built, it became clear that the venture was a financial failure. In 1979, Ginsberg approached Criswell to assist him in preparing the project for sale. Ginsberg's idea was to divide the center into condominium units. In 1980, Criswell agreed to prepare the plans and drafted an agreement which stated:

> I will compile and prepare all information necessary for real estate agents to show and sell the above property on a condominium basis; i.e. to be able to sell each individual building (Building # 1 through Building # 9) as a separate item with necessary information to form an association to accommodate maintenance, taxes, necessary exterior utilities and any other community expenses; *or as a whole project.*
>
> . . .
>
> For the above services, the European Crossroads will compensate to [sic] me at my office, presently in suite # 141, 2829 W. Northwest Highway, Dallas, Texas, a fee of one percent (1%) of the total sales price of each building, buildings, *or entire project* at the time of closing.
>
> Ginsberg signed the agreement on behalf of the limited partnership.
>
> Over the next four months, Criswell compiled data on the shopping center. His primary task was to determine exactly how many square feet were in each unit since various tenants had relocated interior walls over the years. This data was printed in a book at Criswell's expense and several copies were delivered to Ginsberg.
>
> Soon thereafter, Ginsberg asked the center's mortgagee, Clevetrust, for permission to sell the project on a condominium basis. Clevetrust refused, and Ginsberg relayed this information to Criswell. Criswell received no further communications from Ginsberg regarding payment for the book or his services. In 1981, Crossroads sold the entire shopping center under a contract for deed for $12,850,000. It was not until 10 months later that Criswell learned of the transfer. Crossroads refused to pay Criswell his 1% fee.
>
> . . .
>
> Criswell asserted that the agreement was enforceable, whether the center was transferred as a number of separate units of a condominium project, or undivided "as a whole project."
>
> Although it is well settled that the words contained in the instrument, and not the punctuation, should be the controlling guide in construing the instrument, there is no rule which requires courts to disregard all punctuation and look solely to the language of the instrument. Punctuation aids in construing the words used in the instrument. A semicolon is used to mark a more important break in the sentence flow than that marked by a comma. "When items in a series are long and complex or involve internal punctuation, they should be separated by semicolons for the sake of clarity." The language of the agreement

sets out two methods of disposing of the center: first, "on a condominium basis;" or second, "as a whole project." Criswell's use of semicolons in drafting the agreement indicated that each phrase set off by a semicolon was to be read as having independent significance; that is, he used a semicolon to indicate that selling the property "as a whole project" was an alternate and independent means of disposing of the center. This becomes obvious when the language between the semicolons is deleted:

> I will compile and prepare all information necessary for real estate agents to show and sell the above property *on a condominium basis* or *as a whole project.*

In this case, the reasonable interpretation of the agreement is that the phrases "as a whole project" and "or entire project" were parallel expressions of alternate methods of selling the center and were not intended to explain or modify the phrase "on a condominium basis." As a result, we hold that the letter agreement did not require a sale of the shopping center "on a condominium basis" as a condition precedent to Criswell's right to receive compensation.

....

HECHT, Justice (concurring).

....

Rules of construction may be necessary when the meaning of an agreement is ambiguous. This agreement is not ambiguous, and no party contends that it is. The Court's resort to rules of construction, even to the point of straining over the significance of a semicolon, is unnecessary and improper.

....

GONZALES, Justice (concurring and dissenting).

....

While I agree with the court that the cause should be remanded for a new trial, I find it odd that all parties to this dispute, the trial court, the court of appeals, and this court agree that the contract in question is clear as a bell and yet disagree as to its meaning. I would hold that the contract is ambiguous as a matter of law.

....

The court relies upon the significance of the semicolons in the disputed sentence and upon the Chicago Manual of Style but overlooks pertinent law. A semicolon is a mark or point of grammatical punctuation, used for marking off a series of sentences or clauses of coordinate value, "or for the purpose of continuing the expression of a thought, and *never for introducing a new idea.*" Criswell wrote that the shopping center was to be sold "on a condominium basis;. . . ." Arguably, language following the semicolon—"as a whole project"—cannot introduce a new idea, but can only continue the expression that the project be sold on a condominium basis.

Arguments advanced by both parties are rational and both interpretations are reasonable. Thus, I am surprised that the court concludes that the contract is certain and reasonably susceptible to only one meaning.

. . . .

Thus, in my opinion, the trial court committed error in refusing to let the jury decide the true intent of the parties.

Notes and Questions

1. ***Fractured Courts***: There was a majority and dissenting opinion in both decisions above. For each case, consider whether you agree with the majority or the dissent. Why?
2. ***A Consistent Rule?*** Can you define a method for courts to consistently interpret semicolons? Do you think that any such method exists? Could your method explain the outcome in both cases above? Should it be able to? Why or why not?
3. ***Reverse Engineering?*** In your most cynical moments, do you believe that each judge develops a sense of what the "right" outcome is and then finds some basis to interpret syntax and punctuation in a way that supports that view?
4. ***A Deeper Problem?*** You've been reading case after case in which courts struggle to unearth meaning from rambling, complex passages that contain erratic punctuation. Has it occurred to you that there's a deeper problem? From everything that you've read in this book and elsewhere, do you believe that lawyers are truly expert in legal drafting? Have they received adequate training in clear drafting to do their jobs?

   Is it worth your while to seek out a course that focuses on clear legal drafting? Are you in such a course right now? (If so, we applaud you.)

D. Exercises

Each of the sentences below contains a semicolon. Identify those sentences in which the semicolon is used properly.

1. In disparate-impact cases, we focus on the defendant's motivation; not the effects of its actions.
2. The Court of Appeals' decision is discretionary; the issue should not be decided if it would prejudice the other party.
3. To obtain a preliminary injunction, the moving party must show either (1) a likelihood of success on the merits and the possibility of irreparable injury; or (2) the existence of serious questions going to the merits and the balance of hardships tipping in the moving party's favor.
4. We have never squarely addressed whether all temporary shelters fit within the Fair Housing Act's definition of dwelling; nevertheless, we decline to do so here.
5. The names of my dogs are Duke; Renzo; and Roo.

Each of the sentences below contains at least one semicolon. For each sentence, identify whether a semicolon creates ambiguity that makes the sentence susceptible to more than one meaning. If it does, articulate those two (or more) possible meanings.

1. Don't let fears consume you; let your teachers help.
2. Appropriate construction material shall be thatch, lumber, or brick; classified as Grade A and sourced from a pre-approved supplier.
3. §12: The parties agree that neither business shall stock green grapes; nor shall they stock green apples, unless a customer submits a written request and pays a stocking fee.

   [How, if at all, does your answer change if §11 of the contract stipulates that "under no circumstances shall either party purchase, possess, distribute, or sell any fruit that grows on trees"?]

1. Drafting Challenge

You are buying a store that currently sells children's products. The seller, who will be entitled to a percentage of profits after the sale, wants to continue the store's theme as a place to buy children's products. But you'd like to expand to other products. Your lawyer inserts this clause into the purchase agreement:

Buyer shall sell children's clothing; accessories; and footwear.

Is this clause broad enough to allow you to sell products other than children's clothing? Assume you represent the seller and want the store to continue selling only children's products. How could you redraft this provision to ensure that the store is limited to selling just children's products?

TEN

Apostrophe Catastrophe

A. Overview

Apostrophes are curious creatures because they lead double lives.[1] In one life, an apostrophe fills in for letters or numbers omitted from contractions. In its other life, an apostrophe signals that its word is possessive. These examples illustrate the difference:

- *Contraction*: The employee's having dinner in the cafeteria. (The apostrophe is standing in for the *i* in *is*.)
- *Possessive*: The employee's suit is wrinkled. (This is the possessive use—the employee possesses the wrinkled suit.)
- *Plural Possessive*: The employees' uniforms are dirty. (This is the possessive use applied to a group of employees, each of whom possesses a uniform.)
- *No Apostrophe*: The employees meet on Tuesdays. (No apostrophe is needed because this is a plural, not a contraction or a possessive use.)

While this might seem straightforward, it's not. In fact, some grammar and punctuation vigilantes get so riled up about the incorrect placement or omis-

1. Diana J. Simon, The (Not Too Serious) Grammar, Punctuation & Style Guide to Legal Writing 53–67 (2022).

sion of apostrophes in public signs that they sneak around correcting them. One set of vigilantes, armed with Sharpies, went to Arizona and corrected a sign that urged tourists to bring their *camera's*.[2] In Australia, a resident corrected signs advertising *motor's* or services associated with *nail's*.[3]

One employer upped the stakes, going to court over a missing apostrophe. An unhappy Australian real-estate agent took to Facebook to complain that his employer had failed to "pay his employees superannuation." Had the agent placed an apostrophe before the *s* in *employees*, it would have been clear that he was only referring to his own experience. But without the apostrophe, the agent was referring, in the plural, to *all* employees—an allegation that motivated his employer to sue him for defamation. When the agent moved to dismiss the lawsuit, the court refused because the plural use of *employees* made it sound like there was a systematic pattern of conduct.

The moral of the story? Watch your apostrophes, even on social media.

As you'll see below, misplaced apostrophes have sparked or shaped litigation in a variety of contexts, including criminal cases, cases involving wills and other written instruments, and cases involving attorney's fees.[4]

B. In Criminal Cases

A defendant convicted of first-degree murder argued on appeal that his conviction should be reversed because of a misplaced apostrophe. Before trial,

2. Jon Hurdle, *U.S. Typo Vigilantes Correct Errant Signage*, REUTERS (Aug. 23, 2010), https://www.reuters.com/article/us-book-typos-odd/u-s-typo-vigilantes-correct-errant-signage-idUSTRE67M40L20100823.

3. *Anonymous Bristol Resident Wages One-man War on City's Incorrect Signage*, NEWS.COM.AU (April 5, 2017), https://www.news.com.au/lifestyle/real-life/true-stories/anonymous-bristol-resident-wages-oneman-war-on-citys-incorrect-signage-grammar/news-story/ea566b1f3e542c6183257f071bf434f8.

4. Speaking of attorney's fees, this phrase, commonly used among attorneys, is controversial because of apostrophe placement. In fact, one court, which used the phrase "attorney fees" without an apostrophe, found it necessary to explain its approach as follows: "We use *attorney fees* rather than the possessive form *attorney's fees* unless quoting the parties' own documents. Several variations of the term are grammatically correct: *attorney's fees*; *attorneys' fees*; *attorney fees*; *counsel fees*. *See* BRYAN A. GARNER, GARNER'S DICTIONARY OF LEGAL USAGE 94 (3d ed. 2011). Although *attorney fees* may be 'inelegant,' it is 'increasingly common,' operating as 'a means to avoid having to get the apostrophe right.' ... We follow that convention here too." Worsham v. Worsham, 867 S.E.2d 63, 77 n.9 (Va. Ct. App. 2021).

the prosecution represented that it would not use information from the "cellular extractions of *Defendants'* phones" at trial. The prosecution had actually meant to say that it wouldn't use extractions from the "*Defendant's* phone." During trial, the prosecution presented evidence extracted from a co-defendant's phone. The defendant argued that because the prosecution said it would not use the cell-phone extractions of *any* defendant, it had committed a discovery violation warranting reversal.

Wharton v. State

246 A.3d 110 (Del. 2021)

VALIHURA, Justice.

....

B. The Superior Court's[5] *Did Not Otherwise Abuse Its Discretion*

We next address [defendant] Wharton's assertion that the Superior Court erred in not excluding the Incriminating Messages because it should have held the State to its statement in the May 15, 2019 letter that it would not use the *defendants'* cell phone extractions. We first consider whether the State committed a discovery violation based on the circumstances surrounding this letter.

At the time it sent the letter, the State had not yet discovered the Incriminating Messages. The State's prompt action upon discovery suggests no bad faith or misconduct. The trial court carefully considered Wharton's assertions of prejudice and the circumstances surrounding the State's mistaken use of a plural-possessive in the letter. The Superior Court accepted that the misplaced apostrophe was an innocent typographical error and did not constitute a discovery violation. For context, in reaching this conclusion, the trial court noted the "amazing amount of cooperation between the State and the defendant and the voluminous amount of discovery." The trial court also noted that the State had produced discovery that it did not have an obligation to produce to avoid trial by surprise, and that it "applaud[ed] the State's efforts in that regard."

---

5. Ironically, in a case involving a misplaced apostrophe, the court incorrectly used an apostrophe in this heading. There was only a single superior court, so the heading should have read: "The Superior Court Did Not Otherwise Abuse Its Discretion."

Nevertheless, at the hearing on the motion to exclude, the Superior Court ordered time and opportunity for Wharton to conduct two interviews. Wharton did conduct those interviews, but apparently nothing came of them. Although the typo was an unfortunate unintentional mistake, like the Superior Court, we do not believe the State violated its discovery obligations.

....

■ ■ ■

The next case involved the legality of a search warrant. The defendant was convicted for manufacturing amphetamine and was sentenced to 20 years. On appeal, he argued that the trial court erred in denying his motion to suppress the evidence seized from his house because the officers who seized it were in his home illegally. The court of appeals agreed and remanded the case to the trial court. Although the majority didn't focus on the misplaced apostrophe, the concurrence and dissent did:

Burroughs v. State

241 S.W.3d 280 (Ark. Ct. App. 2006)

DAVID M. GLOVER, Judge.

....

[Five or six officers approached a house. The officers admittedly did not advise the woman staying there that she needn't consent to their entry.]

The trial court took the matter under advisement, and in a letter opinion dated April 18, 2005, denied appellant's motion to suppress, specifically finding "that the *officer's* entry into the residence was by spontaneous invitation and not in response to request for consent, so that the provisions of *State v. Brown* do not apply." (emphasis added). Appellant was then subsequently tried by a jury and found guilty. In this appeal, he challenges the trial court's denial of his motion to suppress.

....

A search by any other name is still a search, and this search of the dwelling should have been preceded by advising Ms. Ashmore that she did not have to give consent. Consequently, we hold that the trial court erred in denying appellant's motion to suppress.

LARRY D. VAUGHT, Judge, concurring.

....

Further, and most importantly, the trial court's letter opinion plainly states that "the *officer's* entry into the residence was by spontaneous invitation." (emphasis added). To me, the trial court's use of the singular "officer," and not the plural "officers," is important. It seems logical that when officer Story asked Ms. Ashmore to produce her identification and she responded, "Come in, I'll get it out of my purse," she was inviting only officer Story into the home. Officer Chapmond's testimony, officer Story's testimony, and the trial court's letter opinion support this conclusion.

....

As such, I believe that the "spontaneous invitation" that Ms. Ashmore issued was very limited in scope.

SAM BIRD, Judge, dissenting.

I respectfully disagree with the majority's conclusion that the trial court's denial of appellant's suppression motion must be reversed, and I would affirm the appellant's conviction.

....

I certainly agree with the concurring judge that the majority's position is a "leap" from our supreme court's decision in *Brown.* I do not agree with the concurring judge that the issue presented by this case can be resolved based on the trial judge's placement of an apostrophe in the word "officers" in his letter opinion.

....

[I]t is obvious that [Ms. Ashmore] knew that Lt. Story was not the only law enforcement at the door and that she invited *them* into the house to look in the living room and kitchen. Considering that this testimony clearly establishes that two police officers were in Ashmore's view outside the door, and considering that Ms. Ashmore obviously considered that she was speaking to both of them, it is hard for me to imagine that the trial court, by its use of the singular possessive "officer's" in describing who was spontaneously invited by Ashmore to enter Burroughs's residence, intended to say that the invitation was extended only to Story but not to Chapmond. With all due respect to the trial judge, I cannot agree that this case should be decided on the strength of his understanding of the significance of the location of an apostrophe.... Therefore, I would uphold the trial court's denial of Burroughs's motion to suppress the evidence that was discovered as a result of police entry into the home.

Notes and Questions

1. ***Partial Dismissal?*** An Alabama court's misplaced apostrophe opened the door to an argument that the plaintiffs' suit was still alive against one of two defendants. Both defendants had moved for summary judgment, but the plaintiffs, who were unaware of the hearing, didn't show. The trial court entered an order that stated: "Based on the Plaintiff's failure to appear, the Defendant's Motion for Summary Judgment is granted and this case is dismissed." The plaintiffs argued that the apostrophe's placement signaled a singular possessive, meaning that summary judgment was entered in favor of only *one* defendant. How do you think the court ruled?[6]

C. In Wills and Other Documents

Misplaced or missing apostrophes have also spurred lawsuits involving the interpretation of wills and other documents. In the first case below, the reference in a will to "my brothers children" rather than to "my brothers' children" or "my brother's children" created a family dispute because the decedent had two brothers, both of whom had children.

Money v. Money

176 So. 817 (Ala. 1937)

KNIGHT, Justice.

[Tom Money died and left a will. When he died, he had only one living brother, John Money. His other brother, Jim Money, had already died. Both brothers' children sought the court's aid in interpreting Tom's will. John's children argued that they alone should take under the will, while Jim's children argued that they should be entitled to an equal share. The trial court held that both brothers' living children would inherit equal shares.]

. . . .

The will reads:

. . . .

6. *See* Ex parte Utilities Bd. of Roanoke, 348 So. 3d 1098 (Ala. 2021).

Second. I will that the money from said mortgage goes evenly to my brothers children, and that Malcolm Edmondson share evenly with them, after all expenses including burial and doctor bills are paid.

....

There is no apostrophe before or after the letter "s" in brothers.... And whether he had in mind the children of his living brother only or the children of his deceased, as well as those of his living brother, developed a case of latent ambiguity. Especially is this true when there is nothing to show on the face of the instruments whether the word "brothers" was used in the singular number, in the possessive case, with apostrophe omitted before the "s," or was a plural word, in the possessive case, without the apostrophe following the "s." This latent ambiguity so developed authorized a resort to parol evidence, making admissible the declarations of the testator, and his instructions to the scrivener made and given at, or just before, the time the will was written. [Because it is clear from those instructions that the testator only wanted John's children to inherit, we reverse].

....

■ ■ ■

Much more recently, a missing apostrophe in a construction contract resulted in a $125,000 dispute between a general contractor and a subcontractor. Ultimately, the court held that the missing apostrophe was a "simple error" and ignored it.

Regency Midland Construction, Inc. v. Legendary Structures, Inc.

41 Cal. App. 5th 994 (App. 2019)

WILEY, J.

[A general contractor named Regency hired a subcontractor named Legendary to do concrete work on an apartment building. Legendary quit halfway through, so Regency hired another company to finish the work. That's when Legendary and Regency began feuding about who owed whom what. Regency withheld money from Legendary because the contract allowed Regency to withhold 10% of the amount due Legendary as security to ensure the job was completed.]

....

This summary judgment appeal is purely a duel over contract interpretation, with no disputed issues of fact. The key sentence in the contract between Regency and Legendary specified "Ten percent (10%) of Subcontractor's contract amount shall be withheld and will be released 35 days after completion of subcontractors work." This 10% withholding created the retention sum.

[Supreme Court Justice] Felix Frankfurter reputedly said the three rules of statutory interpretation are to read the statute, read the statute, and read the statute. The same wise counsel applies to interpreting every text. So we read read read the contract, which we now describe.

....

[The disputed provision] reads like this, with our italics: "Ten percent (10%) of Subcontractor's contract amount shall be withheld and will be released 35 days after completion of *subcontractors* work."

The central dispute boils down to the meaning of "subcontractors" in this sentence.

....

Legendary's argument is not crystalline but amounts to this: The italicized word "subcontractors" must mean *any* subcontractor, not just Legendary. Legendary itself did not complete the concrete subcontracting work, true, but the replacement subcontractor ANM did, so once ANM completed the work, Legendary should get the 10% Regency withheld from the payments for the work Legendary did before it abandoned the project. To do otherwise, Legendary protests, is "baseless and inequitable." In sum, then, Legendary says subcontractor should be interpreted to mean *any* concrete subcontractor, not Legendary in particular.

Regency's position, by contrast, is *subcontractor's* work means *Legendary's* work specifically. Legendary's work was the entire concrete job the contract specified—providing all the labor, materials, and equipment and ensuring the result was up to code and free of liens—which Legendary never completed. Thus Legendary is entitled to no further sums. The fact ANM substituted in to save the day does not matter, according to the language of the contract, says Regency.

Regency is right and so was the trial court's result.

As a matter of literal interpretation, Regency wins. The contract defines "SUBCONTRACTOR" as "Legendary Structures, Inc." Legendary's attempt to expand this definition to include ANM violates the contractual language.

[Because the retention language's purpose was to ensure proper performance, and Legendary did not finish the job, it must suffer the consequences of its contractual failing, which is the loss of the 10% withholding.]

Notes and Questions

1. ***A Taxing Statute***: In a New Mexico case, *Estate of Thompson v. O'Cheskey*,[7] a missing apostrophe or comma—neither mark was present, so the court had to decide which was missing—created ambiguity in an estate-tax statute. The statute provided for either a 1% tax or 5% tax on estates. Specifically, it provided that for estates passing to "the spouse, parent or parents lineal descendants, legally adopted child, . . . there is imposed thereon, a tax of one per cent (1%) . . . ." But for "other kindred, . . . there is imposed thereon, a tax of five per cent (5%) . . . ."

   The taxpayers, who were the decedent's niece and nephews, argued that there should be an apostrophe after *parents*. If there were, the niece and nephews, as lineal descendants of the decedent's parents, would be taxed at the lower 1% rate. The Commission of Revenue, however, argued that the phrase should read "parent or parents, lineal descendants" with a comma after *parents*. Read that way, the estate would be taxed at the higher 5% "other kindred" rate because the niece and nephews would not be the decedent's "lineal descendants." The court held that the absence of the comma was a "manifest grammatical error," which it corrected. The taxpayers lost. Later, the law was repealed and changed.

2. ***A Burning Question***: A lease provided that the "Tenant shall pay for any damages . . . caused by any act of negligence of Tenant or any of Tenant's Guests, *except for damage by fire, flood, or other casualty not caused by Tenant(s) guests*." (Emphasis added). One

7. 525 P.2d 894 (N.M. Ct. App. 1974).

of the purported tenants noticed a jack-o-lantern smoking on the front porch. When he tried to remove the candle, it fell, igniting spilled fuel from a kerosene canister also kept on the porch. A fire ensued—and later a multiparty lawsuit involving a fire insurer, college renters, their parents, and the landlord homeowner. The defendants (the tenants) argued that they weren't liable for the fire because the person who caused the fire was a tenant, not a guest. Another party said that the person who caused the fire was not a tenant but a guest. The landlord argued that he meant the clause to transfer liability for fires caused by tenants or their guests. The court described the disputed clause as "indecipherable." How do you predict the court ruled?[8]

3. ***Apostrophe Removal***: In "the case of the missing apostrophe," a plaintiff sued an insurance company called Hartford Lloyd's Insurance Company in state court after his home was damaged by a hailstorm. Later, an entity called Hartford Lloyds (without an apostrophe) tried to remove the case to federal court. The plaintiff argued that the removal was invalid because the entity that removed the case was not a party to the suit. The parties agreed that Hartford Lloyd's and Hartford Lloyds were two different companies and that Hartford Lloyds was no longer in business. How do you think the court ruled?[9]

4. ***A Transformative Apostrophe?*** Tenants living in New York City Housing Authority units funded under Section 9, the federal low-income housing program, brought a class action suit against the Housing Authority for failing to remove mold and excessive moisture from its housing units. The tenants successfully obtained a consent decree requiring the Housing Authority to remedy the mold and excessive moisture. (Consent decrees are court-mandated commitments that "are construed largely as contracts, but are enforced as orders.")

   The Housing Authority failed to fulfill its obligations under the consent decree, so the tenants again sued, securing a revised con-

---

8. *See* Surner v. Appel, 19 Mass. L. Rptr. 454 (Sup. Ct. Mass. 2005).

9. *See* Campbell v. Hartford Lloyd's Ins. Co., 2005 WL 8158547 (Oct. 24, 2005 N.D. Tex.).

sent decree. Before completing the mold abatement, the Housing Authority transferred management of some mold-infested properties to private developers; this also meant that the transferred properties would be funded under Section 8, a different federal low-income housing program. The consent decree did not expressly indicate whether it applied to Section 8 housing, so the parties returned to court to resolve the ambiguity.

The revised consent decree—using the Housing Authority's familiar "NYCHA" initialism without an apostrophe—defined "NYCHA public housing developments" as "public housing developments that receive Section 9 subsidies and are operated by NYCHA." But the defined term only appeared in a section about installation and maintenance of roof fans. The provision requiring the Housing Authority to implement the consent decree used slightly different language, which included a possessive form: "NYCHA shall fully implement . . . this Order across all of *NYCHA's public housing developments* . . . ."

The tenants argued that the possessive *NYCHA's* signaled a departure from the no-apostrophe definition that limited the Housing Authority's obligations to "Section 9" housing. Thus, the tenants argued, the Housing Authority's obligations should include remediation of Section 8 housing, too.

What do you think the court concluded? Was the Housing Authority required to remedy the mold in the Section 8 housing units because of the apostrophe?[10]

D. Attorney's Fees/Offers of Judgment

In the two cases below, apostrophe placement created ambiguity when parties tried to resolve cases through an "offer of judgment." An offer of judgment, codified as Rule 68 of the Federal Rules of Civil Procedure, incentivizes parties to settle by empowering judges to penalize parties that lose after rejecting reasonable settlement offers. When misplaced apostrophes make accepted offers ambiguous, a court may find that there was no agreement.

10. *See* Baez v. N.Y.C. Hous. Auth., 533 F. Supp. 3d 135, 140–41, 144–48 (S.D.N.Y. 2021).

Maffucci v. City of Philadelphia

1999 WL 500021 (E.D. Pa. July 15, 1999)

KELLY, J.

Presently before the Court is Defendants' Amended Offer of Judgment. Two of the three Plaintiffs rejected Defendants' offer, but one, Jean Conti Associates, contends it has accepted the offer, seizing upon the placement of an apostrophe. For the reasons that follow, and in consideration of the hearing the Court held yesterday, the Court finds the offer is ambiguous, and that no mutual manifestation of assent is possible in view of the ambiguity. The Court therefore rejects Jean Conti's position that it has accepted Defendants' offer.

The parties have been involved in various settlement negotiations that culminated with Defendants' offer to all Plaintiffs to settle the case for $215,000.00. As Defendants' counsel explained yesterday, he previously received authority from the City to settle the case for $250,000.00, and, after Plaintiffs declined to accept Defendants' offer, he made an offer of judgment to Plaintiffs for the limits of his authority. Defendants' counsel sent this Rule 68 Offer of Judgment to Plaintiffs twice, although the amended offer did not differ from the original in any material way. The first sentence of both versions substantially read, "[A]ll defendants in the above captioned matter hereby offer to allow judgment to be taken against them by plaintiffs Christopher Maffucci, Selena Fitanides and Jean Conti Associates, in the amount of Two Hundred Fifty Thousand Dollars ($250,000)." The next sentence contains the troublesome apostrophe. "This amount represents the total liability of defendants for any and all of plaintiff's loss, claims, damages, interest, costs...." Because the second sentence refers to the singular "plaintiff," Jean Conti proposes to accept the offer of judgment by itself.

Defendants argue the apostrophe is misplaced, and that this is obvious from the context of the entire offer. Although the word "plaintiff" does not appear elsewhere in the offer in the singular, Jean Conti's position is reasonable, if only barely. In view of this ambiguity, the Court must turn away from the offer's plain language and apply contract law principles to interpret the offer's meaning. These principles require that the parties objectively manifest their mutual assent to the agreement's terms for the agreement to be binding. Those principles also tend to lead courts away from making a client pay for its attorney's mistake.

The requisite mutual assent is lacking here, and the Court finds Defendants are not bound by their offer of judgment. As is evidenced by their offers during settlement negotiations, Defendants never intended to offer any single Plaintiff the amount they were authorized to offer all Plaintiffs. The offer's predominate use of "plaintiffs" supports this view, as does Defendants' use of the conjunctive "and" when referring to Plaintiffs. ... Defendants are not bound by their offer of judgment.

Bradshaw v. Boynton-JCP Assocs., Ltd.

125 So. 3d 289 (Fla. Dist. Ct. App. 2013)

GROSS, J.

....

The offer was apostrophe-challenged, creating ambiguities as to whether the drafter intended references to singular or plural defendants or plaintiffs. The offer, entitled "Defendant's Joint Proposal for Settlement," also appears to have been adopted from a form without sufficient editing; it requires "Plaintiff'(s)" to "execute a stipulation," and "Plaintiff(s)" to "execute" a general release of "Defendant(s)."

In applying [Florida Rule of Civil Procedure] 1.442, the Supreme Court has stated,

> The rule intends for a proposal for judgment to be as specific as possible, leaving no ambiguities so that the recipient can fully evaluate its terms and conditions. Furthermore, if accepted, the proposal should be capable of execution without the need for judicial interpretation. Proposals for settlement are intended to end judicial labor, not create more.

....

The rule requires that "the settlement proposal be sufficiently clear and definite to allow the offeree to make an informed decision without needing clarification. If ambiguity within the proposal could reasonably affect the offeree's decision, the proposal will not satisfy the particularity requirement." ...

Reversed.

Notes and Questions

1. ***Founding Fumbles***: The Framers of our Constitution also struggled with the correct placement of apostrophes. In Article 1, Section 10, clause 2, the Constitution provides: "No State shall, without the Consent of the Congress, lay any Imposts or Duties on Imports or Exports, except what may be absolutely necessary for executing it's [sic] inspection Laws...." Similarly, in Article V, it provides: "or the other Mode of Ratification may be proposed by the Congress:... and that no State, without its Consent, shall be deprived of it's [sic] equal Suffrage in the Senate." Perhaps because most editors prefer not to insert "sic" in the text of our nation's charter, many reprints of the Constitution omit the apostrophe.[11]
2. ***The Politics of Apostrophes***: The possessive use of apostrophes can also have political implications. In Quebec, Canada, some view the apostrophe as a sign of Anglo imperialism against French Canadians, so pressure exists there to omit apostrophes.[12] One court felt compelled to explain its failure to use an apostrophe when referring to St. Marys Portland Cement, a party located near the St. Marys River (also no apostrophe). The court explained that the Geographic Board of Canada in 1898 discouraged the possessive form of place names to avoid suggesting private ownership of a public place. Communities may now use apostrophes if they wish, but the city of St Marys dropped it in 1968 and convinced the cement company to drop it, too.[13]
3. ***The Land of the Apostrophe-free***: Canada is not alone in forming a geographic board. The U.S. Board on Geographic Names, an executive agency that keeps the government's database of official names, has also issued guidelines on apostrophes. One such guideline "discourages" apostrophes in geographical names because the "need to imply possession or association no longer

---

11. *See* Peter Jeremy Smith, *Commas, Constitutional Grammar, and the Straight-Face Test: What if Conan the Grammarian Were a Strict Textualist?*, 16 CONST. COMMENT. 7, 20 n.34 (1999).

12. *See* Maureen Arrigo-Ward, *Caring for Your Apostrophes*, 4 PERSPECTIVES: TEACHING LEGAL RES. & WRITING 14, 15 (1995).

13. *See* St. Marys Cement Inc. v. EPA, 782 F.3d 280, 282–84 (6th Cir. 2015).

exists."[14] Thus, places like Dantes View, Devils Golf Course, and Devils Cornfield, all in Death Valley National Park, bask in the hot sun with no apostrophes.[15]

4. ***Singularly Stern***: One court was so upset by missing apostrophes and other errors in a complaint that it chastised the drafting attorney as follows:

> With callous disregard for the reader, plaintiffs' counsel has done nothing to minimize the confusion in the Complaint and later memoranda.... Despite the presence of two plaintiffs and four defendants, the terms "plaintiff" and "defendant" are often used in the singular, leaving the reader to puzzle out which plaintiff or which defendant is referred to. Similarly, the term "defendants" is often used when counsel does not appear to be referring to all the defendants. And the list could go on—counsel uses possessives without apostrophes, leaving the reader to guess whether he intends a singular or plural possessive. Such sloppy pleading and briefing are inexcusable as a matter of courtesy as well as because of their impact on defendants' ability to respond....[16]

5. ***The Arkansas Apostrophe***: In 2007, a state representative in Arkansas proposed a bill called the "Apostrophe Act of 2007." It declared that the possessive form of the state's name should be *Arkansas's* instead of *Arkansas'*. This sparked a "statewide civil war."[17] Although the issue appears to be unsettled, in 2021, the Arkansas Supreme Court used the apostrophe-*s* approach when referring to "Arkansas's sovereign-immunity doctrine."[18]

---

14. U.S. Bd. on Geographic Names, Version 2.3, *Principles, Policies, and Procedures Domestic Geographic Names* 50 (Dec. 2016).

15. Henry Brean, *Obscure Federal Rule Erased Apostrophes from Place Names*, LAS VEGAS REV.-J. (Feb. 5, 2018).

16. P.M.F. Servs., Inc. v. Grady, 681 F. Supp. 549, 550 n.1 (N.D. Ill. 1988).

17. Paul Greenberg, *An Apostrophe Starts a War*, ARK. DEMOCRAT-GAZETTE (March 4, 2007).

18. Mahadevan v. Bd. of Trs., 633 S.W.3d 756, 758 (Ark. 2021).

6. **Redbook *Sibilant Style***: *The Redbook* is a leading legal-style manual authored by Bryan Garner, a preeminent usage expert. It gives a straightforward rule for signaling the possessive form of a singular noun ending in *s* or *ss*: add an apostrophe-*s* (*'s*). Thus, if you're referring to a single witness's testimony, use *'s*. And if you're writing a book or making a movie called "Bridget Jones's Diary," do the same. But if you're signaling a plural possessive, and the plural noun ends in *s* or *es* (as it usually does), add an apostrophe after the ending *s*. Thus, if you're writing about multiple witnesses, refer to the witnesses' testimony.[19]
7. ***Split Opinions***: Controversies persist, however, about how to use the possessive when a singular word ends in *s*. There are even disagreements among justices of the U.S. Supreme Court. Let's take Kansas as an example. Justices Thomas, Breyer, Ginsberg, and Sotomayor used only an apostrophe when using the possessive of Kansas, while Justice Kagan, when using the same possessive, used an apostrophe-*s*.[20] For an interesting article analyzing the Supreme Court's inconsistent use of the apostrophe-*s* when referring to either proper or common nouns ending in *s*, see Ryan C. Black & Timothy R. Johnson, *Obsessive over the Possessive at the Supreme Court of the United States: Exploring SCOTUS'/SCOTUS's Use of Possessive Apostrophes*, 22 J. App. Prac. & Process 13, 13–14 (2022).

E. Exercises

Identify whether the apostrophes below are correct and whether any are missing. If a sentence is incorrect, correct it:

1. It's clear that the defendant knew that its parking lot was unsafe.

---

19. Bryan A. Garner, The Redbook: A Manual on Legal Style 142 (4th ed. 2018).

20. Kahler v. Kansas, 140 S. Ct. 1021, 1024 (2020) (Justice Kagan, writing for the majority, said the case was "about Kansas's treatment of a criminal defendant's insanity claim"; the dissenting opinion referred to "Kansas' early days of statehood"); Kansas v. Glover, 140 S. Ct. 1183, 1187 (2020) (Justice Thomas, writing for the majority: "[w]e granted Kansas' petition for a writ of certiorari").

2. The plaintiff releases the defendant, Angelica Francombe, and her agents and attorneys.
3. Defendants motion should be denied because he is relying on a two-year statute of limitations that applies to medical-malpractice claims, but this case involves an ordinary negligence claim.
4. The opinion was thoughtful, but it's effects could harm small businesses.
5. Every year, Professor Whitehead leads a group of students on a trip to Washington, D.C., and the students evaluations of the trip are always positive.

■ ■ ■

Let's make it a little trickier. Follow the *Redbook* rules and note whether these sentences are correct or not. If not, how would you correct them?

1. Congress' main role in government is to pass laws and declare war.
2. James and Esme wrote a brief together. James and Esme's brief was persuasive and concise.
3. Paul and Sylvia Jones send holiday cards every year. They always end them by saying, "Best regards, The Joneses."
4. The witness' testimony was boring, but the jury still found him credible.
5. I arrived late for my boss's meeting; she was not amused.
6. The electricians decided to get together and form a union. The electrician's union then worked on getting better wages and other benefits.

■ ■ ■

There's an important exception (also mentioned in the *Redbook*) to the rule calling for an apostrophe-*s* after sibilant endings. Sometimes, a singular entity—such as a court or a business—ends with a plural. In those cases, don't add the apostrophe-*s*. Instead, punctuate as if it were a plural possessive by adding an apostrophe after the existing *s*:

- The court of appeals' decision was controversial.
- Charter Communications' reach is extensive.
- Henkel North American Consumer Goods' website is easy to navigate.

See if that exception applies in either of these sentences:

1. The United States foreign-policy decisions have come under scrutiny this week.
2. The Supreme Court's order summarily reversed the U.S. Court of Appeals decision. [Is this a trick question? Why?]

ELEVEN

Ignoring Poor Grammar and Punctuation

A. Overview

We authored this book in large part to convince you that good style and sound mechanics are essential to your success as a legal writer—as a student and as a lawyer. And as you've seen already, writing lapses can make or break a document or a case. But a bit of counterbalance is in order. We'll use this chapter to show you that, as important as a lawyer's writing is, courts are loath to turn cases upside down over a stray punctuation mark or a shoddy passage. In fact, sometimes improper grammar and punctuation—even when acknowledged—don't even play a supporting role in a court's decision. Sometimes courts ignore these errors altogether.

Why might this be?

This chapter includes (1) a discussion of why courts might disregard improper grammar or punctuation; (2) examples of courts ignoring style errors; and (3) a reminder that regardless of these examples, the modern trend is for courts to care deeply about the impact of improper grammar or punctuation—which means that you should care, too.

B. The History of Ignoring Grammar and Punctuation

Let's begin with the supreme law of the land: the U.S. Constitution. Many scholars argue that punctuation should be ignored when interpreting the Constitution because the Framers were careless about punctuation and used it in ways that are inconsistent with modern practice. For example, many semicolons in the Constitution would likely be commas today.[1] The Framers also had an "annoying habit" of inserting unnecessary commas before the word "shall," thus improperly splitting those sentences' subjects from their verbs.[2] And it's not just the Constitution's original parts—some of its amendments include improper grammar and punctuation, too.

Peter Smith, a constitutional-law expert, offers a telling example of the risks of strictly construing grammar and punctuation in the Constitution. As Smith explains, strictly construing the Twenty-sixth Amendment based on its precise grammatical construction would lead to an absurd result.[3] That amendment, ratified in 1971, lowered the voting age from 21 to 18. But construing it strictly yields a much more dramatic outcome: conferring United States citizenship on anyone who has reached age 18.[4] In other words, the amendment upends the Citizenship Clause of the Fourteenth Amendment, which provides that "[a]ll persons born or naturalized in the United States... are citizens of the United States and of the State wherein they reside."

Here is the key wording of the Twenty-sixth Amendment:

1. Peter Jeremy Smith, *Commas, Constitutional Grammar, and the Straight-Face Test: What if Conan the Grammarian Were a Strict Textualist?*, 16 CONST. CMT. 7, 17–19 (1999); Paul E. McGreal, *There Is No Such Thing a Textualism: A Case Study in Constitutional Method*, 69 FORDHAM L. REV. 2393, 2406 (2001) ("The existing evidence suggests that the drafters either ignored the significance of punctuation or used semi-colons much as we use commas today."). But *see* David S. Yellin, *The Elements of Constitutional Style: A Comprehensive Analysis of Punctuation in the Constitution*, 79 TENN. L. REV. 687, 691 (2012) ("[M]any scholars... argue that the Framers were extremely careful with their language.... [P]unctuation must be dealt with squarely and cannot merely be explained away as the product of careless authorship.").

2. Smith, *supra* note 1, at 18.

3. *Id.* at 7–13.

4. *Id.* at 7–8.

> Section 1. The rights of citizens of the United States, who are eighteen years of age or older, to vote shall not be denied or abridged by the United States or by any State on account of age.

Can you see what the problem is? If your answer is the use of a nonrestrictive clause instead of a restrictive clause, you are correct. A nonrestrictive phrase or clause "is one that could be taken out of the sentence without changing the essential meaning."[5] It merely "adds information about the person, thing, or idea to which the phrase or clause refers."[6] When you include a nonrestrictive clause, the phrase should be set off with commas.[7] (*The judge, who seemed eager to move to the next case, was harried and irritable.*)

On the other hand, a restrictive clause adds information "that is essential to identify the noun it attaches to, and it is not set off with commas."[8] (*The lawyer who hired her was once a partner at my mother's firm.*)

By setting off the phrase "who are eighteen years of age or older" with commas, the Framers used a nonrestrictive clause. Thus, a strict grammarian would conclude that because the clause only further defines who is a citizen of the United States, it defines the entire class of United States citizens as people who are 18 or older.[9] Of course, no one intended to repeal the Citizenship Clause of the Fourteenth Amendment, and no one has argued that due to this grammatical error, anyone 18 or older is a United States citizen.[10]

The drafters of this amendment should have used a restrictive clause—a clause that "adds information that is essential to identify the noun it attaches to."[11] Again, such a clause is not set off by commas.

How could the amendment have been revised to reflect what Congress meant? One option:

---

5. Bryan A. Garner, The Redbook: A Manual On Legal Style 7 (4th ed. 2018).

6. William Strunk & E.B. White, The Elements of Style 4 (4th ed., Longman 1999).

7. Redbook, *supra* note 5.

8. *Id.*

9. Smith, *supra* note 1, at 10.

10. *Id.* at 11.

11. Redbook, *supra* note 5, at 7.

> The rights of citizens of the United States who are eighteen years or older to vote shall not be denied or abridged by the United States or by any State on account of age.[12]

Of course, even this construction isn't perfect—it uses passive voice, among other issues. (Leading off with "The voting rights of United States citizens who are eighteen years or older" might make it clearer still.)

The point is that proper grammar is not always a predictable indicator of constitutional construction, and interpreters usually ignore improper grammar when the history and purpose of a clause or provision dictate otherwise.[13]

The same logic applies to statutory construction more generally. One theory underlying why punctuation should not carry the day in construing statutes is that "in days of yore, it was held that because many legislators voted only on the basis of bills that they heard read aloud—without seeing the printed page—they could take no notice of the punctuation marks."[14] But even recently, the Alabama Supreme Court ignored a statute's punctuation, borrowing this passage from an 1880 case that did the same:

> It is the language, the words of the statute, which must be construed, without indulging in criticisms upon its grammar, or its punctuation. Statutes in the course of legislative procedure are read to the General Assembly, and, as is said, they apprehend them by ear, not by the eye, which alone can take cognizance of punctuation....[15]

The recipe for the "ignore punctuation and grammar" approach also includes a dash of classism and a pinch of sexism. Historically, punctua-

---

12. Smith, *supra* note 1, at 12.

13. For a history behind the ratification of the Twenty-sixth Amendment, see Smith, *supra* note 1, at 7–8. There are many similar examples in the Constitution. For example, the Presidential Eligibility Clause, if read literally, would disqualify every president after Zachary Taylor as president. Yellin, *supra* note 1, at 698–99.

14. Antonin Scalia & Bryan A. Garner, Reading Law: The Interpretation of Legal Texts 161 (2011). Even today, however, while you might think that it is members of Congress that draft legislation, that is not true. The Legislature's understanding of a bill typically is based on short memoranda and oral briefings they receive from staff. These sources do not address the smaller details of statutory text, which generally are left to staffers. For an in-depth article that discusses how Congress passes statutes today, see Jesse M. Cross, *The Staffer's Error Doctrine*, Harv. J. on Legis. 83, 84 (2019).

15. Deutsche Bank Nat'l Tr. Co. v. Walker Cnty., 292 So. 3d 317, 327 (Ala. 2019) (quoting Danzey v. State, 68 Ala. 296, 298–99 (1880)) (cleaned up).

tion was deemed unimportant because it was thought to be "the work of the engrossing clerk and printer."[16] In other words, learned sophisticates couldn't be bothered.[17]

The historical distaste for punctuation among privileged men also stems from the view that using correct punctuation is a "feminine" trait.[18] In a 1923 article, a male lawyer wrote that most lawyers don't care about punctuation, instead leaving it to the "temperamental mercies" of the stenographer.[19] Most stenographers were (and perhaps still are) women, and, in that author's words, using punctuation is "essentially feminine."[20] Instead of a "rugged and bold reliance on words to convey meaning, which would be the masculine way of doing things," lawyers let their stenographers dress sentences "with the lace and ruffles of punctuation."[21]

Today, it's easy to recognize these views as dated and preposterous, though classism and misogyny have by no means vanished from the legal profession. The most effective lawyers recognize that the law is language. Far from "niceties" to be fobbed off on others, precise and accurate grammar and punctuation are tools in the successful lawyer's belt, strengthening credibility and persuasiveness—and thus increasing the likelihood of favorable outcomes.

So how does ignoring punctuation and grammar play out in court opinions? In the first Supreme Court case addressed below, the Court ignored a grammatical error and a punctuation defect when interpreting a federal statute involving common carriers.

---

16. Reading Law, *supra* note 14, at 161 (quoting Morrill v. State, 38 Wis. 428, 434 (1875)). *See also* Danzey v. State, 68 Ala. 296, 298–99 (1880) ("It is most often the work of the draftsman, and not infrequently of the clerk entrusted with the duty of copying or of the printer in publishing.").

17. One court went even so far as to suggest that courts should shy away from "grammatical niceties" because "as our work product attests, judges and lawyers are not grammarians. No one looks to the bench and bar for grammatical guidance.... We are as likely to err in technical grammatical matters as anyone else who lacks expertise." TPG (Post Oak) Acquisition, LLC v. Greystone Multi-Fam. Builders, Inc., No. 01-18-00396-CV, 2021 WL 3870130 (Tex. App. Aug. 31, 2021), *review granted, judgment vacated*, and *remanded by agreement*, No. 21-1120, 2022 WL 18935634 (Tex. Apr. 1, 2022).

18. Richard C. Wydick, *Should Lawyers Punctuate?*, 1 Scribes J. Legal Writing 7, 9–10 (1990).

19. *Id.*

20. *Id.*

21. *Id.*

C. Statutory Cases

The Supreme Court has a long history of downplaying or sidestepping grammatical errors in statutes. In *Barrett v. Van Pelt*,[22] the Court noted a litany of errors and didn't hide its dim view of Congress's drafting efforts. The Court explained that the "language and structure of the second clause is so inapt and defective that it is difficult to give it a construction that is wholly satisfactory."[23] Specifically, the statute read "damaged" where Congress had obviously meant "damage."[24] This error, the Court noted, "makes a grammatical defect and embarrasses interpretation."[25] The statute also included an errant comma that made no sense.

But the Court ignored these errors, giving effect to Congress's seeming intent instead of engaging in a "too rigid adherence to the very word and letter of the statute."[26] The Court emphasized that punctuation is a "minor, and not a controlling element in interpretation, and courts will disregard the punctuation of a statute, or re-punctuate it, if need be, to give effect to what otherwise appears to be its purpose and true meaning."[27]

You might be thinking that the 1925 *Barrett* case reflects the time in history when "lowly" clerks were charged with punctuating statutes and male lawyers were writing articles about how punctuation was a woman's job, equivalent to adding adornments like lace and ruffles. But courts have relied on *Barrett*'s reasoning in more recent decisions.[28]

For example, in 1989, the Supreme Court justices sparred over the presence of commas around a critical phrase in the Bankruptcy Act of 1978.[29] The majority held that its reading of the statute was mandated by the statute's

---

22. 268 U.S. 85 (1925).

23. *Id.* at 88.

24. *Id.* at 90.

25. *Id.*

26. *Id.*

27. *Id.* at 91 (internal quotations omitted).

28. In fact, it has been cited and relied upon as recently as 2022. United States v. Dion, 37 F.4th 31, 37 (1st Cir. 2022) (citing Barrett v. Van Pelt, 268 U.S. 85 (1925)). In citing *Van Pelt*, the First Circuit said that "we will not accord decretory significance to omissions in punctuation." *Id.*

29. United States v. Ron Pair Enterprises, Inc., 489 U.S. 235 (1989).

"grammatical structure."[30] The four dissenting justices, however, questioned the significance of a "capricious" bit of punctuation whose usage is "exceedingly arbitrary and indefinite."[31] The dissent cited *Barrett*, among other authorities, for the proposition that "[p]unctuation is not decisive of the construction of a statute."[32]

Similarly, in 2009, the Massachusetts Supreme Court ignored a comma in a state statute involving airline fees for curbside baggage services.[33] After addressing the grammatical structure of the provision and the errors in it, the Court declined to interpret the statute based on its punctuation.[34] Quoting *Barrett*, it belittled the comma: "[T]o paraphrase a statement attributed to Sigmund Freud, sometimes a comma is 'just' a comma."[35]

Likewise, a dissenting Kansas Supreme Court justice questioned whether the Kansas Legislature even follows "esoteric rules of punctuation" in drafting statutes: "Kansas legislative specification regarding comma usage is relatively thin.... Let not any essential meaning hinge on a comma...."[36]

D. Contract Cases

Like the decision in *Barrett v. Van Pelt*, an 1837 Supreme Court case involving an early land-ownership dispute helped to spread the idea that punctuation is irrelevant in interpreting written documents of all kinds. In *Ewing's Lessee v. Burnet*,[37] in response to one party's argument about punctuation, the Court opined that "[p]unctuation is a most fallible standard by which to interpret a writing: it may be resorted to, when all other means fail."[38]

---

30. *Id.* at 235.

31. *Id.* at 249–50 (O'Connor, J., dissenting) (cleaned up).

32. *Id.*

33. DiFiore v. Am. Airlines, Inc., 910 N.E.2d 889 (Mass. 2009).

34. *Id.* at 896.

35. *Id.* at 896–97.

36. Glaze v. J.K. Williams, LLC, 439 P.3d 920, 926 (Kan. 2019) (Rosen, J., dissenting) (cleaned up).

37. 36 U.S. 41 (1837).

38. *Id.* at 54.

Later courts borrowed that language and ran with it. For example, in 1930 the Iowa Supreme Court interpreted a contract's assumption clause.[39] The dispute centered on the presence of a semicolon, and the Court agreed that the semicolon created ambiguity but stressed, citing *Ewing's Lessee*, that punctuation was "of little aid in construing it."[40] The Court went even further, proclaiming that "[p]unctuation is no part of the English language."[41]

Similarly, in 1967 the Colorado Supreme Court faced a peculiar passage in an insurance policy. A sentence preceding a vertical list ended with a period instead of a colon.[42] The result was that if read literally, the insurance policy didn't cover anything: "This insuring agreement does not apply."[43] The court ignored the "offending" period and explained that punctuation does not control the construction of a contract, especially because there is "still much uncertainty and arbitrariness in punctuation."[44]

Even though the cases above are on the older side, some recent cases repeat these propositions. In 2007, a North Carolina appellate court stressed that "punctuation or the absence of punctuation in a contract is ineffectual to control its construction as against the plain meaning of the language."[45] And in 2012, a New York court recited what it termed a "cardinal principle" of contract interpretation: "mistakes in grammar, spelling or punctuation should not be permitted to alter, contravene or vitiate manifest intention of the parties as gathered from the language employed."[46]

---

39. Seeger v. Manifold, 231 N.W. 479 (Iowa 1930).

40. *Id.* at 480.

41. *Id.* at 481.

42. McKinley v. Colo. Farm Bureau Mut. Ins. Co., 431 P.2d 859 (Colo. 1967).

43. *Id.* at 860.

44. *Id.* at 861 (internal quotations and citation omitted). The Supreme Court of Louisiana also took this view when construing an offer to buy land, stating that "in construing contracts, we are not as much concerned with the niceties of grammar... and the technicalities of punctuation." Weingart v. Delgado, 16 So. 2d 254, 256 (La. 1943).

45. CB&H Bus. Servs., L.L.C. v. J.T. Comer Consulting, Inc., 646 S.E.2d 843, 844 (N.C. Ct. App. 2007).

46. Banco Espirito Santo, S.A. v. Concessionaria Do Rodoanel Oeste S.A., 100 A.D.3d 100, 109 (N.Y. App. 2012).

E. Ignoring Grammar and Punctuation in Wills

When it comes to wills, and especially handwritten "holographic" wills, courts have been quick to ignore punctuation and grammatical errors. For example, in *Estate of Carter v. Carter*, the court determined that issues such as the spacing, paragraph breaks, punctuation, and capitalization in the will were not reliable guides in determining intent.[47] The court held that it had "the right and duty to disregard" these errors.[48] Similarly, in *Clayton v. Burch*, the North Carolina Supreme Court stressed that it could "disregard improper use of capital letters, punctuation, misspelling and grammatical inaccuracies, especially where the will is written by an unlearned person."[49]

F. Circling Back: Grammar and Punctuation Do Matter

Although this chapter presents the other side of the story regarding mistakes in grammar and punctuation, as you saw in earlier chapters, you needn't look far to find many more cases—and many more recent cases—revealing the hazards of sloppy work.

The current view is perhaps best reflected in the book *Reading Law*, authored by late Supreme Court Justice Antonin Scalia and leading usage expert Bryan Garner. It explains the most important principles of constitutional, statutory, and contractual interpretation. Scalia and Garner underscore that "[n]o intelligent construction of a text can ignore its punctuation."[50] And judges, often citing the book, agree.

For example, in 2018 the Texas Supreme Court focused squarely on grammar and punctuation in construing a statute.[51] The Court stated that "[p]unctuation can be helpful, and even determinative, when construing statutes and other

---

47. 404 S.W.2d 693, 696 (Mo. 1966).

48. *Id.*

49. 80 S.E.2d 29, 31 (N.C. 1954). In contrast to statutes and contracts, it is more reasonable to ignore punctuation and grammar because the person creating the will might not have the technical skills and, more importantly, is not present to explain their intent.

50. READING LAW, *supra* note 14, at 161.

51. Tex. Health Presbyterian Hosp. of Denton v. D.A. & M.A., 569 S.W.3d 126, 131–33 (Tex. 2018).

written texts."[52] Citing Scalia and Garner's book, it emphasized that "[l]ike punctuation, grammar rules can be crucial to proper construction."[53]

The U.S. Court of Appeals for the District of Columbia Circuit was equally adamant about the importance of grammar and punctuation when it interpreted a federal statute in 2014.[54] The court flatly rejected the plaintiffs' argument, based on *Barrett,* that it should ignore the statute's punctuation. The court explained that the Supreme Court's 90-year-old *Barrett* decision was decided long before the development of modern approaches to statutory interpretation.[55] And the court dismissed the notion that grammar and punctuation can be ignored when searching for meaning in language:

> The idea that we should entirely ignore punctuation would make English teachers cringe.... Congress communicates through written language, and one component of written language is grammar, including punctuation.... Put another way, "all of our thoughts can be rendered with absolute clarity if we bother to put the right dots and squiggles between the words in the right places."[56]

Anyone aspiring to success in the legal profession will do well to remember the D.C. Circuit's words—and will note modern courts' close attention to the style and mechanics of legal language.[57] While historically lawyers might have gotten away with a document that disregards proper grammar and punctuation, such an approach is very risky today. Take it from scholars, lawyers, and judges: these components, far from being "lace and ruffles," are key components of language. And lawyering is, in large part, about using language effectively.

52. *Id.* at 131.

53. *Id.* at 132.

54. NACS v. Bd. of Governors of the Fed. Res. Sys., 746 F.3d 474, 486 (D.C. Cir. 2014).

55. *Id.*

56. *Id.* (quoting Lynn Truss, Eats, Shoots & Leaves 201–02 (2003)).

57. *E.g.*, Diaz v. North Star Tr., LLC, 481 P.3d 557, 564 (Wash. Ct. App. 2021) ("We employ traditional rules of grammar in discerning the plain language of the statute.... A legislative body's use of a verb tense holds significance in construing statutes.").

Table of Principal Cases

Index